THE WORLD'S BOMBERS

PUTNAM WORLD AERONAUTICAL LIBRARY

THE WORLD'S
BOMBERS

H. F. KING

THE BODLEY HEAD

LONDON SYDNEY TORONTO

ISBN 0 370 01554 1
© H. F. King 1971
Printed and bound in Great Britain for
The Bodley Head Ltd
9 Bow Street, London WC2E 7AL
by Cox and Wyman Ltd, Fakenham
Set in Monotype Baskerville
First published 1971

CONTENTS

ACKNOWLEDGMENTS

The extracts on pages 18–21 are printed by permission of Dodd, Mead & Company Inc., New York, and are from *The Story of the Winged-S* by Igor I. Sikorsky. Copyright 1938, 1941, 1948, 1958 and 1967 by Dodd, Mead & Company Inc.

The photographs appearing in this book were kindly supplied by the Boeing Company (page 99); Consolidated Vultee Aircraft Corporation (78); Convair Division, General Dynamics Corporation (96, 101); *Flight International* (71); P. L. Gray (26); Lockheed (77); Ministero della Difesa-Aeronautica, Italy (31, 63); the Glenn L. Martin Company (58); North American Aviation Inc. (79); Short Brothers and Harland Ltd (15); John W. R. Taylor; VFW-Fokker (90).

INTRODUCTION: AN EXCLUSIVE GATHERING

The main classes of military aircraft are fighters and bombers, but although a comparatively few bombers have been successfully adapted for use as night fighters a great number of fighters have made excellent bombers – of a kind.

Should a definition of 'bomber' be required in respect of the present volume this might be 'An aeroplane designed or adapted for the primary purpose of delivering a bomb or bombs in level flight against non-specialised targets over medium and long distances.'

However, there can be very few types of aircraft from which bombs could not be dropped in time of emergency or for particular purposes. Even helicopters have been used in Vietnam for discharging small bombs, or grenades. Thus a very common class of aircraft today is the fighter bomber, an aircraft having the usual characteristics of a fighter but designed or adapted to carry bombs or other offensive weapons for use against surface targets. This class of aircraft is sometimes called a tactical fighter, close-support fighter, or strike fighter, and among the most advanced examples is Britain's Hawker Siddeley Harrier, which is capable of taking-off and landing vertically.

Together with other classes of aircraft which are, or have been, used for bombing, the fighter bomber is not dealt with in this book. The other classes omitted include the specialised dive-bomber, or one which delivers its load in a steep diving attack with the aid of special equipment, notably braking surfaces to restrict its speed. The best known dive-bomber of all was the German Junkers Ju 87 Stuka. The dive-bomber would be better considered together with the fighter bomber and with another class of machine, specialised like itself, designed for ground attack or assault with bombs and other weapons but having no special diving equipment. The finest example of such an aircraft was the Russian Stormovik.

Still another class of aircraft used for bombing has been the torpedo-bomber, or one designed to drop a load of bombs as an alternative to a torpedo. Most machines of this class have been intended to operate from aircraft carriers, and a well-known specimen is the Grumman Avenger. Yet another class which, like the torpedo-bomber, finds no place in the present review is the patrol bomber, or maritime reconnaissance aircraft, a long-range type which can also number the bomb among its armoury of weapons and of which the finest example today is perhaps the Hawker Siddeley Nimrod. In the past such aircraft have frequently been large seaplanes or flying-boats.

A final class to be excluded is the utility or economy ground-attack machine which can operate with bombs. This is often related to a trainer and is well exemplified by the British Aircraft Corporation Strikemaster, though there are far simpler and cheaper types.

Such aircraft as these are best reserved for review in another volume which could be entitled *Strike Aircraft*, the word 'strike' being generally taken to signify the attack of targets in support of the army or navy, using bombs among other weapons.

Lest it be supposed that by making the present gathering an exclusive, rather than an inclusive, one the scope is unduly restricted, it must be noted that the number of types reviewed in the following pages is a large one, and as most of the aircraft concerned are themselves large, and complicated accordingly, all available space will be required to do them justice. The variety of their design is no less diverse than is the case with fighters, and certain types which are little known, though used in war, receive due treatment.

Definitions of terms which may be unfamiliar are given as the narrative proceeds, but the present occasion is taken to explain the contractions used in the tables at the end of each descriptive chapter. Thus: r-c m-g = rifle-calibre machine-gun; that is, one having a calibre, internal measurement of the barrel, or bore, approximating to that of a standard military rifle of the period (commonly 7–8 mm or 0·303 in). h m-g = heavy machine-gun, or one of about $\frac{1}{2}$-in calibre. c = cannon, a gun of 15-mm calibre or greater, usually capable of firing explosive shells.

The term 'service ceiling' means the height at which the rate of climb has fallen to 100 feet a minute. The heading 'armament' signifies in this instance defensive armament. Offensive armament, in the form of bombs, is not given, for this would have little meaning unless related to range, or distance over which the load could be carried. Bomb loads and ranges are quoted at intervals in the text, however, so that a progressive indication is given of bomber efficiency.

It cannot be too strongly emphasised that figures quoted for weight, speed and service ceiling are mere approximations. Factors which could strongly influence such figures include the quantities of bombs and fuel demanded for a particular sortie, mission, or operational assignment; these, in turn, would depend on the distance to be flown, the nature of the target, and the direction and strength of the wind. One other important consideration is the reliability and completeness of surviving information, for secrecy often prevailed while military aircraft were still in service and figures later issued often lacked authority.

These explanations having been given, it must first be related how the specialised bomber grew from types of aircraft never designed for bombing.

1

Pressed into Service

In the ancient Greek legend which tells of aerial attacks by Perseus upon Medusa and a sea monster no mention of bombs occurs; but the hero was equipped with a polished shield which enabled him to watch his intended victims without looking directly at them, and this may well be related to the radar devices carried by modern bombers to 'see' their targets at night or in bad weather.

Bombing was certainly foreseen by Father Francesco de Lana in Italy during 1670. Having described an airborne invasion by soldiers, he wrote of iron weights being hurled from the air to wreck ships at sea, of the setting of ships on fire with 'fireballs or bombs', and the destruction by similar means of houses, fortresses and cities.

The difficulties of bombing from, or with, a balloon were, of course, great, for a balloon can only travel with the wind. Nevertheless, in 1849 the Austrians launched against Venice small unmanned paper balloons filled with hot air and carrying time-fused bombs weighing 30 lb. A bomb is said to be time-fused when its fuse, or the device which causes it to be, or makes it ready to be, exploded, is adjusted to function after a certain passage of time. Devices of this kind were widely used in later years. On one occasion the Austrian 'flying bombs' (for such they really were) are said to have pursued their launching crews.

With the coming of dirigible, or steerable, airships, notably the German Zeppelins, practical bombing became a very real and frightening possibility. The early employment of these craft in warfare was, however, disastrous, for three Zeppelins were shot down by gunfire within three weeks of the German

◀ Like a number of other French bombers, the Voisin pusher biplane was not a thing of beauty, but it gave excellent service.

invasion of Belgium. These craft were operating by day, and the Germans quickly learned to use the cover of darkness for protection. Later the dark-painted night-bombing aeroplane established itself as an entirely new factor in warfare.

Although it is here assumed that a bomb is a container for explosive or incendiary material it is worth noting that the word derives from bombada, a catapult weapon used by the Romans for hurling missiles against the walls of cities. The catapult was succeeded by the cannon, or large gun, and the bomber aeroplane is often, and quite correctly, likened to a long-range gun.

The term 'bomber' is British, and came into general use during the First World War as a companion to 'fighter'. It has since been adopted by America, though there was a time when the Americans frequently called their bombers bombardment ships. In France the bomber is an avion de bombardement, in Italy an apparecchi da bombardamento, in Germany a Bombenflugzeug, though in the Second World War the type was generally known to the Germans as Kampfflugzeug (battleplane) and the German bomber squadrons were called Kampfgeschwader.

There is a belief among historians that the first man to drop dummy bombs from an aeroplane was the great American designer/constructor Glenn Curtiss, the date quoted being 30 June 1910. The present writer believes otherwise, for there is clear evidence that during January 1910 the French pilot Louis Paulhan carried in his Henri Farman biplane Lieut Beck of the United States Artillery 'in order that experiments might be made in the dropping of dummy bombs'. There may have been earlier experiments, but it seems fairly certain that the first 'live' bombs were released almost exactly a year later from a biplane designed by the Wright brothers. The pilot was P.O. Parmalee and the bombs were released by Lieut Myron S. Crissy of the US Army.

The first known instance of bombs being dropped from an aeroplane in actual warfare occurred on 1 November 1911, during the war between Italy and Turkey. The pilot concerned was Italian, and it will later be shown that Italy played an important part in the development of the bomber aeroplane.

It soon became clear that in order to drop bombs with any degree of accuracy a form of sight, or aiming device, would be necessary, and one of the earliest bombsights was that installed in a Wright biplane by Lieut R. E. Scott, US Navy, during 1912. It was reported at the time: 'The marksman, who in this case is the inventor of the apparatus, lies on his chest between the pilot and the motor and has a view of the ground through a mica window in the fore portion of the housing.'

There are four points of particular interest concerning this early installation by Lieut Scott. The first is that the aeroplane used was of the pusher type, having the engine and airscrew, or propeller, behind the pilot and passenger. This allowed the bomb-aimer (or bombardier as he eventually became known to the Americans) to have an unobstructed view for his activities. This same characteristic of the pusher type of aeroplane enabled a gun to be freely used. The second point was that Scott adopted the prone position, though this has more than once been claimed as an innovation made by a Royal Air Force pilot about ten years later. Thirdly, the American inventor/bomb-aimer was protected from the rush of air and took his sight through a window, as on bombers of later years. Last, the bombs were carried horizontally beneath the aeroplane (this was likewise to become common practice) and not dropped overboard as was usual.

At the Paris Salon in December 1913 another remarkable bombing installation was on view. This was the work of Henri Coanda, and the aeroplane concerned was a Bristol tractor biplane, or one having the engine and propeller at the front. In this instance the bombs were carried internally, or largely so, so that their drag, or air resistance, could have little effect on the speed of the aircraft. A contemporary report explained: 'A bomb-dropping apparatus, set in the floor of the fuselage, and consisting of a cylindrical drum on which are mounted twelve cigar-shaped bombs, is worked from the observer's seat by means of a small lever.' For the same type of aeroplane an elaborate bombsight was designed; yet when war came in August 1914 there were no aeroplanes specially equipped for bombing.

Special aircraft bombs had been designed and made and small stocks of these were available, but in general the situation was confused, and even chaotic. Writing of his early days as a mechanic in the Royal Flying Corps, one of Britain's greatest fighter pilots, Maj J. T. B. McCudden, vc, recalled of his arrival in France: 'Forthwith we started to fit little wooden racks to carry small hand grenades, which were to be used as bombs, because at the commencement of hostilities we had nothing in the way of aerial bombs of any sort whatever. We also received some flechettes, or steel darts. . . . We dropped a lot of these, but I never heard whether they did much harm.' Describing the situation a short time later McCudden added: 'At this time the RFC's principal work was reconnaissance and bomb-dropping, our bombs still being hand and rifle grenades, and also petrol bombs, which consisted of a gallon of petrol carried in a streamlined canister which was ignited on impact with the ground.' And a little later still:

'We were now receiving fairly large size bombs for disposal. One type, which was painted red, weighed ten pounds, and had a small parachute attached to give it directional stability; it was called a shrapnel bomb. Another new type was really a converted French shell, and was afterwards condemned as being highly unsafe. I mention these types of bombs because they were our early attempts at producing this very necessary adjunct to aerial warfare.'

As with bombs, so with aeroplanes, it was a matter of making use of what was available. In the book *The World's Fighters* it is related how a tiny single-seat biplane called the Sopwith Tabloid, built before the 1914 war for sporting and scouting purposes, was among the first British types to be adapted for fighting; but in this rôle it achieved very little success, because the tractor class of aeroplane, to which it belonged, was poorly suited for the mounting of guns. As a bomber the Tabloid quickly achieved one tremendous success, in one of the earliest raids of the war.

The story is one of a victory following close on the enforced withdrawal of British forces from Antwerp on 7 October 1914. The last two aeroplanes to leave the Belgian city were two Tabloids, flown by Sqn Cdr Spenser Grey and Flt Lieut R. L. G. Marix. These two officers were ordered to bomb the Zeppelin sheds at Cologne and Düsseldorf and they

took-off on 8 October. Mist prevented Spenser Grey from bombing the sheds at Cologne and he dropped his bombs on the city's railway station. Marix had better fortune: from 600 ft his bombs fell upon the shed at Düsseldorf. There was a great explosion and flames leaped 500 ft high. The brand-new Zeppelin L.IX and its shed had been destroyed.

Hardly less dramatic and spectacular was the raid on 21 November 1914 by three Avro 504 tractor biplanes on the Zeppelin sheds at Friedrichshafen. One of the Avros was shot down, but a Zeppelin was badly damaged and a gasworks was destroyed.

Both these raids were made by the Royal Naval Air Service, and it was that same service which pioneered strategic bombing, intended to cripple the enemy's war effort by bombing munitions factories, transport centres and similar targets behind the lines. This method of employing bomber aircraft was a major factor in the winning of the Second World War and must be differentiated from tactical bombing, or bombing in the battle area in support of ground forces.

During the opening weeks and months of the war several types of aeroplane were pressed into service as bombers. The Tabloid and the Avro 504 have already been named. Other Sopwith types were similarly adapted, as were machines made by the

With its wing span of 85 ft, the Short Bomber (page 37) of 1916 was among the largest aircraft in existence, although it had only one engine. The tiny Eastchurch Kitten experimental fighter (span 19 ft) gives scale.

Bristol and Martinsyde companies. Early types of B.E.2, designed at the Royal Aircraft Factory, Farnborough, also carried bombs, as did Short landplanes and seaplanes. The Germans made early raids with monoplanes of the Taube type; but special notice must be taken of the French Voisin pusher biplanes, for these quickly became established as more-or-less specialised bombers. The first of these in service was the Voisin Type L, which, having an engine of only 80 hp, could lift only a small load of bombs. If any aircraft could be claimed as the first specialised, or 'real', bomber to go into service, this might be named as an improved type known as the Voisin III, having a 120 hp Canton-Unné water-cooled engine. Of this type well over 2,000 were built, and supplied not only to France, but to Belgium, Russia, Great Britain and Italy. The type was used for fighting as well as bombing, but by May 1915 France possessed four bomber groups, each composed of four squadrons, and all equipped with these sturdy Voisin weight-lifters.

The bomber had now arrived.

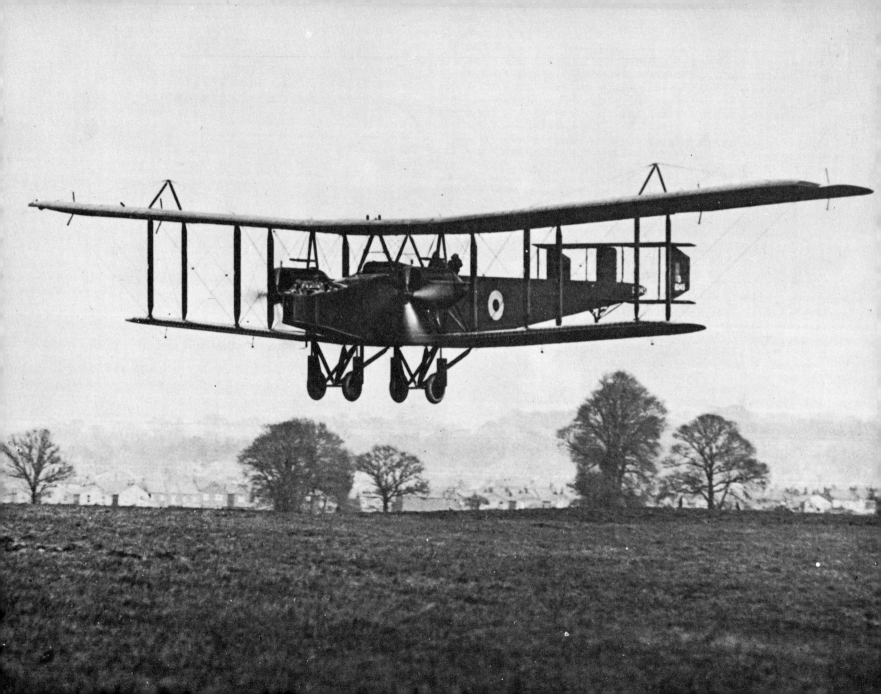

2

The First Big Bombers

'At Um el Surab the Handley stood majestic on the grass, with Bristols and 9A like fledglings beneath its spread of wings. Round it admired the Arabs, saying, "Indeed and at last they have sent us THE aeroplane, of which these things were foals." '

Thus, in *The Seven Pillars of Wisdom*, did Lawrence of Arabia recount how his Arabs viewed a twin-engined Handley Page bomber standing with smaller single-engined types.

There are many romantic stories, legends and beliefs concerning Britain's Handley Page bombers. Many are true, but others are far from the truth. Certainly untrue, as will later be shown, is the claim that the Handley Page O/100 was the first big bomber, or the first successful big bomber. Equally untrue are the assertions that the German Gotha was modelled on the O/100 and that the four-engined

V/1500 was the first bomber to have a gun in the tail.

Although the Handley Page family of bombers, which began with the O/100 late in 1915, and continues today in the RAF's Victor, is an historic one, the world's first big bomber was beyond doubt Russian. The story of how this bomber came into being may be given in the words of its creator. This man is Igor Sikorsky, whose name is further honoured in the volume *The World's Helicopters*. Mr Sikorsky's use of the expression 'ship' for 'aeroplane' is explained by the fact that he has worked for many years in America.

Having recorded the building of the *Grand* and *Il'ya Muromets*, the world's first large four-engined aeroplanes, the ordering by the Russian Army of ten machines of the second type, and the entry of Russia into the war of 1914, Mr Sikorsky wrote:

◀ Two of the famous Rolls-Royce Eagle engines provided power for the equally famous Handley Page O/400.

Igor Sikorsky's Il'ya Muromets was the world's first four-engined bomber. Its size is indicated here by Russian soldiers.

'The holiday atmosphere of the successful flights of the *Il'ya Muromets* was forgotten. I now had not only hard work to do but also the responsibility of training and checking out Army pilots who were to receive the ships and proceed to the Front. This was my work during the day, because at that time I had been, for more than a year, the only pilot in the world to fly four-engined ships. While many fliers, and particularly Lavrov and Prussis, were familiar with the controls of the *Il'ya Muromets* in the air, yet none except myself attempted to take-off or land the big ship. During the evenings I worked at the factory, completing the first five planes ordered by the Army, and installing armament, bomb racks, and other military equipment. Later in the night I worked at home developing a new type of large plane, especially designed for military purposes.

'At that time none of my ships had participated in military flights. I realised that the huge planes with roomy cabins, but with low speed and limited altitude, would not be successful for actual war purposes. Working late in the night, undisturbed by visitors or the telephone, I was developing in a hurry a preliminary project of my third type of large airplane, to be known as the "Military *Il'ya Muromets, Type V*". The ship was not as large, and lighter, and it had a much smaller fuselage, and one single cabin properly arranged for bombs and military equipment.'

The building of this first specialised bomber has a double interest which has never, perhaps, been fully appreciated. First, it had four engines, and early in 1915 it was delivered to the Eskadra Vozduchnykh Korablei (Squadron of Flying Ships) which had been established in December 1914. The first bombers built outside Russia which could be described as big were three-engined Italian Capronis, which did not enter service until August 1915, and even this was well· before the first experimental Handley Page O/100 was completed. The second point of special interest concerning the *Il'ya Muromets* bomber is that it was developed from a type (the *Grand*) which had been designed to carry passengers in great comfort, whereas, it is explained in the volume *The World's Airliners*, the first big passenger-carrying aeroplanes to enter service after 1918 were conversions of wartime bombers.

Mr Sikorsky was not only ahead of designers in other countries but truly ahead of his time. The historic story of his activities in 1914 may be resumed in his own simple words:

'Early in October I received a call from a Colonel of the Army Artillery Service.

' "Will you take me up in the *Il'ya Muromets* one of these days? We want to test some new bombs on the proving ground near Petrograd. It will be more convenient to use the large ship because the bomb racks are not yet ready for the new bombs."

' "Of course, Colonel, I shall be glad to arrange the flight."

'On the same afternoon he came back to the airport with a small Army delivery truck which carried the cases of bombs.

' "Let us take six of the forty pound bombs and one of eighty," said the Colonel.

'The cases were opened on the ground and then carried into the plane.

' "We shall screw in the fuses before each bomb is dropped."

'I looked inquisitive and he went on to explain.

' "The fuses on this type of bomb are extremely sensitive, and even a minor shock would cause the projectile to explode. Once the fuses are in, however, until the small propeller here at the rear of the bomb is unscrewed, the whole is harmless and can stand substantial shock without exploding." '

Mr Sikorsky goes on to describe how four of the 40-lb bombs were successfully dropped through an opening in the floor and how Lieut Lavrov flew the aeroplane while he himself went back into the cabin to watch the dropping of the next bombs. The small ones went overboard successfully; then the Colonel asked Sikorsky to help with the big eighty-pounder. It was bumpy in the air and the two men had difficulty in getting the bomb out of its case and carrying it towards the opening. On the way they laid it on the floor while the Colonel screwed in the fuse. Then the bomb was lifted again towards the opening. As the men approached, a gust of air struck the tail of the bomb – and the little propeller began to whirl. Sikorsky continues:

'A moment later it fell out under our feet! Both the Colonel and I realised what that could mean. We looked at each other, and without saying another word started to move toward the opening. I do not believe that a sick child was ever carried more gently and tenderly than we carried that huge bomb with the safety screw out.'

After more tense moments the bomb was persuaded overboard, and Sikorsky concludes:

'We looked at each other again and smilingly congratulated ourselves. Some sixteen seconds later the bomb struck the ground, and produced a huge explosion with a big, bright red flame and a black cloud of smoke. A few seconds later the sound of the shock, together with the air wave, came up. We could easily hear it, in spite of the noise of the engines, and we could easily feel the shock against the bottom of the cabin, although the ship was at that time more than 4,000 feet high.'

The great Russian designer/pilot may thus be considered not only to have pioneered the bomber but to have assisted in a very personal capacity in developing its armament.

The name Il'ya Muromets was retained for a whole family of bombers of somewhat differing types, and these were armed with machine-guns, firing from the sides of the fuselage. If an enemy fighter attacked from directly astern a signal was made to the pilot to turn sharply, so that the gunners could open fire; but if the bomber was near its target the sudden manoeuvre spoiled the bomb-aimer's chances. Accordingly, officers of the Squadron of Flying Ships worked out a scheme for mounting a machine-gun in the extreme tail of the fuselage, and Sikorsky himself made the necessary design alterations to enable the installation to be made.

A tail gun position was a feature of many bombers used in the Second World War, and the gunners who manned these became known as 'Tail-end Charlies'.

Igor Sikorsky's early experience of bombs, bombers and bombing extended even further. A small German bomb once landed near him, and he was able to record: 'It was so close that I could reach the hole without even getting on my feet. It was about three feet wide and one and a half feet deep . . . I put my hand down in the still warm earth at the bottom, and found several pieces of the bomb, which I took away as souvenirs.'

Had Sikorsky been standing on his feet, instead of lying down prone when he heard the bomb coming, the course of bomber development might have been otherwise, not to mention the development of the helicopter and flying-boat. As for the development of bombs, Sikorsky's 'huge' 80-pounder may be contrasted with Britain's 22,000-lb Grand Slam 'earthquake' bomb, the heaviest dropped in the Second World War.

A little-known fact is that the first production-type Il'ya Muromets Type V, or IM-V, bombers had British engines. These were eight-cylinder water-cooled Sunbeams of 150 hp each. The engines of the next version, the IM-G1, were in some instances Sunbeams and in others of German Argus type.

Machine-guns were mounted not only to fire through doors and windows but from 'crow's-nest' positions in the centre of the top wing; an additional gun fired under the fuselage. Compared with earlier aircraft of the type, the wing area and consequently the lifting capacity, was increased by giving the wings a greater chord, that is, by increasing the distance from the front, or leading edge to the trailing edge.

First of the IM series to have the tail gun position, of the type already mentioned, was the G2; this version also had a gun in the nose. The engines were now of Russian type, having six cylinders arranged one behind the other, as had the German Argus. Engines so arranged were described as inline types, whereas those having cylinders arranged in the form of a V when viewed from front or rear (end-on) were said to be of V or vee type. Such an engine was the Sunbeam already mentioned. The six-cylinder Russian engine was sometimes called the Russobalt, and the next version of the Il'ya Muromets, the IM-G3, was sometimes known as the Renaultbalt. This was because two of the engines were of the French Renault vee type whereas the other two were of Russian type. In this version the maximum bomb load had increased to about 2,000 lb, and the bombs could be carried either vertically or horizontally. Various structural weaknesses were experienced in the earlier IMs and the G4 was stronger.

The last members of this remarkable series of bombers will be dealt with in the following chapter.

The 'father' of the Italian Caproni bombers, which come second in place only to the Russian Sikorskys, was the Ca 30 of 1913. This had three French Gnome air-cooled rotary engines, of 'catherine wheel' type, one mounted centrally as a pusher, the other two driving indirectly two tractor propellers. The indirect drive was not satisfactory, and on the Ca 31, which flew at the end of 1914, two of the engines, as well as the propellers they drove, were moved outboard, that is to port and starboard (left and right) of the centreline of the aeroplane. These engines were mounted at the front of two slender fuselages, sometimes called booms, although that term is more generally applied to the pole-like members supporting the tails of single-engined pusher types.

The first Caproni bomber to be produced in quantity for the Italian Army Air Service was the Ca 32, with three Italian Fiat inline water-cooled engines each of 100 hp. Deliveries of this type began in August 1915 and continued throughout 1916, towards the end of which year the Ca 33 went into production. This version had two additional wheels under the nose of the central nacelle, or short fuselage. At the rear of this nacelle and above it was a sort of birdcage structure, open at the top to allow a gunner to stand inside and work a machine-gun, mounted above the top rail. The gunner must have been a hardy fellow.

It was a great compliment to Caproni that the Ca 33 was built under licence in France.

The long succession of Britain's Handley Page bombers had its origins in a specification issued by the Admiralty in December 1914. A specification, as implied in this instance, is a document which specifies, or states, requirements, and the essential requirements were for a twin-engined bomber suitable for operating for long periods over water with six 100-lb bombs. Mr (later Sir) Frederick Handley Page came forward with proposals for a large biplane with two 120 hp Beardmore engines. Having examined these, Commodore Murray F. Sueter, Director of the Air Department of the Admiralty, encouraged 'H.P.' to think along even more ambitious lines. What he really wanted, he said, was a 'bloody paralyser' of an aeroplane. The two men understood each other, and the paralyser materialised late in 1915 as the O/100.

It had been intended that the new bomber should have two 150 hp Sunbeam engines, but as construction progressed so did work on two new Rolls-Royce engines, which were to become famous as the Eagle and the Falcon. Both these engines were of water-cooled twelve-cylinder vee type, and by the summer of 1915 the larger one, which was to become the Eagle, had proved capable of delivering no less than 300 hp. For early tests in the air, however, it was thought prudent to take no more than 250 hp from the engine, and with some 500 hp at its disposal the first O/100 took the air during December 1915.

Several modifications, or alterations, were made as experience was gained: the cabin enclosure for the crew, with its bullet-proof glass and armour plate, was taken off and armour was removed from other parts. Changes were also made in the tail unit, and by November 1916 the first O/100s were ready for service. Two were delivered safely to the 5th Wing of the Royal Naval Air Service at Dunkerque, in France, but the third landed by accident twelve miles behind the enemy lines. The Germans, of course, studied their prize with great thoroughness; but the common belief that their famous Gotha bombers were modelled on the British machine is, as already mentioned, false.

Most of the first raids by O/100s were made in daylight, but on the night of 16/17 March 1917 a single machine attacked the railway station at Moulin-les-Metz. After one of these precious bombers (for they were few in number) was shot down in daylight the type was confined to operations by night. U-boat bases, industrial and railway centres and airfields (or aerodromes, as they were then called) all received the attentions of the big Handley Pages, and four were withdrawn to England for anti-submarine patrols over the North Sea. In June 1917 a single O/100 made a remarkable flight from England to the island of Lemnos in the Aegean Sea. Stops were made in Paris, Rome and the Balkans, and while crossing the Albanian Alps at a height of 10,000 ft the water in the radiators used for cooling the engines froze. On 9 July 1917 this same O/100 dropped twelve 112-lb bombs on the Turkish capital of Constantinople (now Istanbul), but on a second attempt it experienced engine failure and came down in the Gulf of Xeros. The crew, including the pilot Flt Lieut J. Alcock, whose name will appear in later pages, were taken prisoner.

The flight of the O/100 from England to Lemnos was an early instance of a ferrying flight, that is, a transferal from one centre of operations to another. In later years it became customary to quote for bombers not only a range (distance which could be flown) with bomb load, but also a ferry range, or range attainable with extra fuel instead of bombs.

With various modifications, notably the moving of the fuel tanks from behind the engines to the fuselage, the O/100 became the O/400. The standard, or normal, engine for this type was the Rolls-Royce Eagle VIII of 360 hp, but demands for this excellent engine were heavy, and installations were made of less powerful Eagles, 320 hp Sunbeam Cossacks, 275 hp Sunbeam Maoris, 260 hp Italian Fiats and 350 hp American Liberties.

The O/400 was certainly one of the most famous and successful big bombers of the 1914–18 war, and merits description in some detail.

The fuselage was built in three sections, a central portion, where the bomb bay, or bomb compartment, was located, and nose and tail sections. The crew consisted of one pilot, one or two rear gunners, and an observer, who also acted as bomb-aimer and front gunner. The bombs were aimed by means of a sight mounted externally on the extreme nose of the fuselage. Immediately behind, on top of the fuselage, was a Scarff ring-mounting carrying one, or sometimes two, Lewis machine-guns. The bombs were released by means of cables. Behind this nose position was a cockpit having two seats side by side, and the observer/front gunner/bomb-aimer could gain access to the hinged left-hand seat through an opening in the bulkhead, or transverse partition, separating the two compartments. Near this left-hand seat was a second set of bomb releases for emergency use. These two forward stations, or crew positions, were reached through a triangular door in the bottom of the fuselage.

The bomb bay occupied the lower part of the next, central, part of the fuselage. Above were petrol tanks. Sixteen 112-lb or eight 250-lb bombs could be carried in the bomb bay, suspended vertically by the nose, each in a separate cell, as in a honeycomb. The bottom of each cell was covered by a door, which was opened by the weight of the falling bomb and closed again by a spring.

In the tail section of the fuselage, close behind the central part, was a second gunner's position. Sometimes there were two Lewis guns here, each mounted on a bracket on the port and starboard side; in other instances there was one gun, on a rocking-pillar, or rocking-post mounting, pivoted at its base but capable of being displaced from side to side. There were two firing platforms, or fire-steps, one on each side. Another Lewis gun could be fired backwards and downwards through a trapdoor in the floor. The guns were carried not only for defence but to shoot-up ground targets, including searchlights.

After entering service the O/400 was adapted to carry heavy bombs, which were too big to go in the bomb bay, underneath the fuselage. Possible loads were three bombs of about 500 lb or one of 1,650 lb. When one of the 1,650-pounders was dropped on Wiesbaden on the night of 23/24 October 1918 the destruction was so great that the inhabitants thought it was caused by a group of bombs joined together.

Friedrichshafen has already been associated with Zeppelins and a British air raid. It can now be

Undoubtedly one of the finest bombers of the First World War was the high-flying Gotha G V. Severe raids on London were made by this type.

further associated with big German bombers. These had their origins in a twin-engined pusher biplane, the Friedrichshafen G I, built in 1914. During 1915 the G II appeared, and this entered service in small numbers late in 1916. More widely used was the G III, a larger and more powerful development with two 260 hp Mercedes D.IVa six-cylinder water-cooled inline engines. This type of engine was certainly among the best produced during 1914–18. Construction of the G III airframe – the aeroplane less its engines and equipment – was interesting because the fuselage had a steel-tube framework, covered with wood at the front and rear and with fabric over the central part. Equally interesting was the use of steel-tube spars, or main transverse

structural members, in the inner portions of the wings. The wings were covered partly with wood and partly with fabric. In addition to four main-wheels and a steel-shod skid, or runner, under the tail, there was a fifth wheel under the nose. This was a precaution against nosing over in the event of a bad landing. About a ton of bombs could be carried.

Friedrichshafen G IIIa and G IV bombers also entered service. The G IIIa had a biplane, instead of a monoplane, tail unit; the G IV was of tractor, instead of pusher, type. Having no cockpit in the nose it was also shorter.

The famous Gotha biplanes were generally similar in design to the Friedrichshafen types just mentioned. The two earliest versions, the G II and G III, were not produced in great numbers, but the G III was notable not only in having the excellent Mercedes D.IVa engines, but in having a very remarkable armament installation, which was retained on later Gothas, Viewed from the side, there was no evidence of anything unusual. In the nose of the fuselage was the customary gunner's cockpit, with a Parabellum machine-gun on a ring-mounting. Behind the wings, on top of the fuselage, was a second machine-gun station. What was not obvious was that this station was associated with a special plywood-lined tunnel which allowed the gun to be sighted and fired rearwards and downwards through the fuselage, thus

Germany's Zeppelin Staaken Giants were aptly named. The only version built in quantity was the R.VI, as shown. It had a wing span of over 138 feet.

affording protection against fighters attacking from behind and below.

In the autumn of 1916 the Gotha G IV appeared, and it was this version which took over from the Zeppelins the German long-range bomber offensive. In reaching their targets the Gothas depended not only on their defensive armament of machine-guns but also on their ability to fly at high altitudes, even with bombs aboard. The ceiling, or maximum height attainable, was over 20,000 ft. This was attributable in part to the qualities of the Mercedes D.IVa engines, but also to the high aspect ratio of the wings. Aspect ratio is defined as the ratio of the span, or breadth, to the chord, a term already

explained. Thus, a wing of high aspect ratio, which is efficient in the attainment of high altitude and long range, is great in span and short in chord.

London is the target most generally, and most correctly, associated with the Gotha bombers. During the first half of 1917 special squadrons were being equipped for the systematic bombing of England, and on 25 May twenty-three bombs fell on Kent. More raids were made in June and August and hundreds of casualties were sustained in London. Public concern became grave and fighters were withdrawn from France to strengthen the defences.

Night attacks on London began in September 1917. A typical load was six bombs of 110 lb. In December of that year the Gothas were joined by Zeppelin Staaken Giants, of a type later described, and on the night of 19/20 May 1918 43 Gothas and Giants struck at the capital. Considerable damage was inflicted, but three of the bombers were claimed by anti-aircraft guns and three by fighters. London was then left alone.

The night raids by the German bombers made a very deep impression on the memories of those who experienced them. Shortly after the Armistice a man living just east of London wrote:

'It was generally agreed that the aeroplane raids were far more nerve-racking than those by Zeppelins, and it was seldom, too, that those raids were relieved by a sight of the raiders, although their unwelcome presence in our vicinity was distinctly evident by the ominous and unmistakable drone of their engines. Occasionally, however, a searchlight would discover an enemy plane, and then would follow a terrific bombardment from guns whose proximity was totally unknown to the general public. Now and again, too, machine-gun fire in the air, and occasionally a display of explosive bullets, would indicate a fight going on between aeroplanes.'

London will not forget the Gothas. They became so notorious, indeed, that it was commonly believed that all big German bombers were Gothas, just as it was thought that all German airships were Zeppelins.

There were, in fact, other German twin-engined bombers in addition to the Friedrichshafen and Gotha types. These were made by the A.E.G. company and differed widely from the others, being smaller and more compact and having tractor, instead of pusher, propellers.

The A.E.G. bombers had their origins in a twin-engined biplane called K.1 and built early in 1915. This type was later redesignated G I, and it may now be explained why all the German bombers so far mentioned have had a designation prefixed by the letter G, irrespective of manufacturer: with typical thoroughness the Germans decided to classify all such aircraft by the name Grossflugzeug (big aeroplane).

The A.E.G. G II was built in small numbers as a bomber, as was the larger G III, which carried 660 lb of bombs. The version built in the greatest quantities, however, was the G IV, which had two Mercedes D.IVa engines, a steel-tube fuselage and a bomb load of 770 lb. This was a light load compared with that of, say, the Handley Page O/400, but, as noted, the A.E.G. bombers were relatively small, and their comparatively short range suited them more for tactical than strategic bombing.

France was relatively late in developing large twin-engined specialised bombers and the first of these was the Letord 3 of 1917. This, and other aircraft of the same family, was designed by Col Dorand of the French Service Technique and was built by the Letord company which had been formed in 1908 to manufacture balloons and airships. Characteristic of the Letord 3, 5, 7 and 9 night bombers was the backward stagger of the wings, that is, the placing of the lower wing ahead of the upper wing. The Letord 5 was a sesquiplane, or one-and-a-half-winger. This was built in some numbers, but the Letord 9 existed only as a prototype (first model, experimental or pattern aircraft), for at about the time of its construction the French Government had decided to standardise, or adopt as normal squadron equipment, the Farman F.60 Goliath. Farman had earlier produced the F.50 bomber, which resembled the German Gothas though it was of tractor type. Few F.50s were built, and the Goliath was too late for the war.

	Span	Length	Crew	Loaded weight	Maximum speed	Armament
RUSSIA						
Sikorsky IM-G2	100′ 3″	56′ 1″	4	11,680 lb	72 mph	4 r-c m-g
ITALY						
Caproni Ca 33	72′ 10″	35′ 9″	4	7,300 lb	94 mph	2–4 r-c m-g
GREAT BRITAIN						
Handley Page O/400	100′ 0″	62′ 10″	3–4	13,360 lb	97 mph	3–5 r-c m-g
GERMANY						
Friedrichshafen G III	77′ 11″	42′ 2″	3	8,680 lb	88 mph	2–3 r-c m-g
Gotha G IV	77′ 9″	40′ 6″	3	8,760 lb	87 mph	2 r-c m-g
FRANCE						
Letord 5	59′ 3″	36′ 8″	3	5,390 lb	99 mph	2 r-c m-g

3

Bigger Bombers

The largest Il'ya Muromets of all was the IM-Ye2, which had a wing span of just over 113 ft and weighed more than 15,400 lb when loaded. During 1917 this aircraft was armed with a 50-mm cannon, in addition to eight machine-guns; but only one example was built. There was a slightly smaller type, the IM-Ye1, the wing span of which was about 10 ft less. Six of these were completed.

Although the fitting of armour plate for the protection of the crew or vulnerable parts of an aircraft was by no means unknown during the 1914–18 war, special mention must be made of a form of armour protection with which experiments were made in connection with the big Sikorsky bombers. The plating was 10 mm thick and was made from metal shavings pressed together. Even more remarkable, self-sealing fuel tanks were deve-loped, these, as their name implies, being able to seal the holes caused by gunfire.

Armour protection and self-sealing fuel tanks were important features of the bombers used in the Second World War.

The story of Handley Page bomber development may now be resumed by recording that in November 1917 an O/100 was flown with four engines. Two engines were carried between the wings on each side of the fuselage. The engines forming each pair were arranged in tandem, or one behind the other; the front engines drove tractor propellers, the rear pair acted as pushers. This installation was purely experimental, but it provided valuable information for the design of a far bigger Handley Page bomber, the V/1500, which had its four engines similarly arranged.

The Handley Page V/1500 had a wing span of 126 feet and was intended for the bombing of Berlin and other German centres.

For the new bomber, which was truly a giant, having a wing span of 126 ft, a new type of Rolls-Royce engine was intended. Named Condor, this was really an enlarged development of the Eagle; but it was not ready in time for the V/1500, the first example of which flew with four Eagles in May 1918.

The V/1500 was intended for attacks on Berlin and other German centres, and as it was recognised that long periods would have to be spent over enemy territory, exposed to fighter attack, heavy defensive armament was provided. The most notable development in this connection was the provision of a gun position in the extreme tail of the fuselage, as on some bombers of the Il'ya Muromets type. The technical significance of this was that the gunner would have a

wide field of fire, or could use his gun freely without fear of hitting part of his own aircraft. He was, of course, very vulnerable to enemy fire; on the other hand he had a better chance of surviving a crash than his fellow crew-members. This soon became clear when the first V/1500 crashed on an early test flight and was completely burnt out. The only surviving crew-member was the occupant of the tail gun-position.

The bomb load of the V/1500 could consist of up to thirty bombs of 250 lb; but an alternative load was one or two bombs of a new type weighing no less than 3,300 lb. Nevertheless, the point made earlier concerning bomb load and range was well illustrated in the case of this huge bomber. Assuming

A massive bomb is seen in place beneath the bottom wing of this Caproni Ca 42 triplane. It has two fuselages and a central nacelle.

that it would operate from an aerodrome in Norfolk, near England's east coast, its bomb load for a raid on Berlin would probably not have exceeded 1,000 lb, having regard to the great quantity of petrol.

The 'Super Handley', as the V/1500 became known, was ordered into production to the extent of 255 machines, but only three were ready for action at the Armistice. The 'Berlin Bomber', as it was also called, was never required for its intended purpose.

Over twelve feet longer in wing span than the V/1500 were Germany's Zeppelin Staaken Giants, of the type which, as recorded in the preceding chapter, were used in company with Gothas for raids on London. But sheer size was not the only

remarkable aspect of these monsters. For instance, they were unusual in that even some of the experimental prototypes were used on active service. The first of the line was the V.G.O. I, which had three 240 hp Maybach engines and was first flown as early as April 1915. The V.G.O. II was similar, but insufficient power was provided by the three engines and the V.G.O. III had six Mercedes engines each of 160 hp. The arrangement of these engines was remarkable. In nacelles, or housings, on each side were two engines in tandem, driving not tractor and pusher propellers as on the Handley Page V/1500, but acting solely as pushers. Even more remarkable, the fifth and sixth engines were mounted side by side in the nose of the fuselage and drove a single tractor propeller.

The R IV was mainly similar to the V.G.O. III, and the change in its designation is explained by the fact that the Germans had now decided to class such aircraft by the name Riesenflugzeug (giant aeroplane). The earlier types were redesignated accordingly. The R V had a single engine in the nose, but in the R VI, which was the only version to be built in quantity, the nose-mounted powerplant was abandoned. Instead there were four Maybach or Mercedes engines in tandem pairs between the wings. The nose was now free for the mounting of a machine-gun, and from this position also the eighteen internally stowed 220-lb bombs were released. So great was the weight that the undercarriage had eighteen wheels, two of which were under the nose.

In terms of wing span the German Giants were the biggest bombers used in the 1914–18 war; but they were not the tallest, for this distinction goes to certain members of the Italian Caproni Ca 40/43 series. This is explained by the fact that these were triplanes, though they followed the general layout of the earlier Caproni biplane bombers, having two slender fuselages, or booms, and a central nacelle, or body. Small numbers of Ca 40s and 41s were built, but the most widely used version was the Ca 42. An unusual feature of this type was that it carried its bomb load, which could total about 4,000 lb, in a container attached to the bottom wing.

These huge Caproni triplanes performed well, but were slow and vulnerable, and Caproni reverted to the biplane layout for the Ca 44/47 series of bombers. The bestknown of the series was the Ca 46, which was variously fitted with 250 hp Isotta-Fraschini, 300 hp Fiat or 400 hp Liberty engines. The Ca 46 was an excellent bomber, and was built not only in Italy but in France and the USA also. Handley Page O/400s were also built in the USA, but the first bomber of original American design has yet to appear in this account.

	Span	Length	Crew	Loaded weight	Maximum speed	Armament
GREAT BRITAIN						
Handley Page V/1500	126′ 0″	62′ 0″	6	24,700 lb	97 mph	3–5 r-c m-g
GERMANY						
Zeppelin Staaken R VI	138′ 6″	72′ 6″	7	25,265 lb	81 mph	6–7 r-c m-g
ITALY						
Caproni Ca 42	98′ 1″	49′ 6″	5	16,535 lb	87 mph	4 r-c m-g
Caproni Ca 46	76′ 9″	41′ 5″	4	11,685 lb	94 mph	2–4 r-c m-g

4

Smaller Bombers, Faster Bombers

There have been numerous attempts in the past to classify bombers according to weight or bomb load (light, medium or heavy); the distance they could fly (short-, medium- or long-range); the altitude at which they approached their targets (high-, medium- or low-level); and the number of engines fitted (single- or multi-engined). These attempts have generally been of only passing significance, for bombers in the main have shown marked operational flexibility, or adaptability in use. That the two preceding chapters were devoted to 'big' bombers, as distinct from the smaller types, is merely explained by the fact that the big bomber was early to develop, far earlier, in fact, than is commonly supposed. But although some of the first bombers were large machines there were many smaller types which served in the 1914–18 war which remain to be

mentioned, and certain of these are of great significance.

Among these smaller machines were the French Voisins, briefly introduced in an earlier chapter. Some of the names bestowed upon these sturdy, cumbersome but serviceable biplanes are perhaps better left unrecorded; but among these was 'chicken coop'. As already noted, the Voisins were well established in service by May 1915. Their sturdiness was partly due to the extensive use of steel in their construction. They were able to operate from small, rough fields, and they were certainly among the first aeroplanes to be fitted with wheel brakes, which enabled their short landing run to be reduced even further. There were numerous versions, sometimes distinguished by a makers' designation and sometimes by one decreed by the French War

Ministry. The last of the line were the Voisin X and XI, known to the company as the LAR and E94 respectively. These were considerably larger than earlier bomber versions, having a wing span of nearly 60 ft. The Voisin X was the commonest, and the first of these entered service early in 1918. They were used as night bombers and were painted black accordingly. A bomb load of 660 lb could be delivered on a target about 150 miles distant.

In the early stages of the war some pusher biplanes of Farman type were used for dropping bombs. A few Henri Farmans of steel construction were supplied to Britain's Royal Naval Air Service, and four of these were sent to the Dardanelles. One of the most famous of RNAS pilots, Cdr C. R. Samson, has left record of a remarkable exploit in one of these machines. Writing of December 1915 he said: 'On the 18th I took up a 500-lb bomb on a Henri; this was by far the biggest bomb that up to date had been dropped from an aeroplane in the war. The Henri took it up like a bird, much to my delight. I searched round for over half an hour looking for a suitable target, but there seemed to be a lack that day of objectives worth while. Finally, I selected a long building from which smoke was appearing, deciding it must be full of Turks. I let go the bomb and turned round to see the result, but to my chagrin a cloud blotted out the ground . . . It was only in 1919 that

I saw the results. I had scored a direct hit; the building, which was about 60 ft long, was absolutely wrecked. . . .'

Other types of pusher biplane used by the French for bombing were designed by Breguet and built by Michelin. One of these, the BM V, resulted from a specification issued by the French Ministry of War during 1915 and calling for a bomber capable of destroying enemy munition factories. A bomb load of 660 lb was required, and the specified range (to the target and back) was 370 miles. It may be noted here that the distance over which a bomber can deliver its load and return to its base is called its radius of action, or operational radius.

A point of interest concerning the early Breguet-Michelin bombers is that they were designed as pushers at the request of the French Chief of Staff. This was in order that they could be easily recognised by friendly anti-aircraft gunners, for the Germans were using aircraft only of tractor type. The pusher, however, was inevitably slower than a comparable tractor machine by reason of the drag, or air resistance, created by the booms which carried the tail, together with their associated bracing, or stiffening, struts and wires. The drag created by the wing structure was also high, for these early pushers were commonly of three-bay type, having three pairs of bracing struts between the wings (interplane struts) on each side. So profuse were the struts and wires that it was jokingly said at the time that if a bird were placed between the wings and escaped then some of the bracing wires, which comprised the rigging, were missing, and the aircraft was not safe to fly.

The French constructor Louis Breguet, however, had been one of the earliest to build tractor aeroplanes, and late in 1916 test-flights were made with the prototype of a two-bay tractor biplane which, in bomber form, and designated Breguet 14 B2, was to become one of the most famous of all French bombers. The significance of the suffix B2 was that the aircraft was a bomber with a crew of two. A typical load was 32 bombs, each one of 22 lb. This load would be written in a technical document as 32×22-lb. The maximum speed was over 112 mph and the range 435 miles.

So successful was the new Breguet bomber that it was ordered into production at several factories, and in 1918 the main Breguet works alone was enlarged to allow a production rate of four machines a day. A larger three-bay development, having a bomb load of 1,322 lb, was built in numbers as the Breguet 16 B2, but it was the earlier machine which remained in general service after the war, even as late as 1930.

Two-seat tractor biplanes used by the Germans for bombing were the Albatros C III, C VII and C X, Aviatik C III, Halberstadt CL II, Hannover CL IIIa, L.V.G. C II and Rumpler C I. In November 1916 an L.V.G. C II made the first daylight raid on London; the first night attack on the English capital was made by an Albatros C VII at about one o'clock on a morning in May 1917. Five 22-lb bombs were dropped. Although a height of about 13,800 ft was attained on the run-in to the target the Albatros made the actual attack in a glide, with the engine switched off. The object of this was to surprise the defenders.

Although the F in their designations signified that they were originally designed as fighters, and although they served with distinction in that capacity, the British F.E.2b and F.E.2d single-engined pusher biplanes were very widely and successfully used as bombers, especially at night. The night raids began late in 1916, and during the following year heavy attacks were made on German industrial targets and communications. To make these attacks more hazardous the Germans supplemented their anti-aircraft guns with balloon barrages, or groups of captive balloons, with the mooring cables of which it was hoped the bombers would collide in the dark. In January 1918 an F.E.2b was indeed brought down by such a barrage and experiments were made with fenders, to fend off, or deflect, the balloon cables. These devices were not adopted for general use until the Second World War.

A typical load for the F.E. bombers was two bombs of 112 lb, but three such bombs were occasionally carried. Alternative loads were one 230-lb or twelve or more 20-lb bombs. The bombs were sighted by the pilot, using a sight fixed to the side of the nacelle.

Among the British tractor biplanes used for bombing were the Short Bomber and the Sopwith 1½ Strutter. The Short machine was developed from a seaplane and was fitted with a four-wheeled undercarriage in addition to a tailskid. For a single-engined machine it was very large, the wing span being no less than 85 ft. Short Bombers gave good service until the arrival of the Handley Page O/100. The two-seat version of the Sopwith 1½ Strutter was used for bombing with the load carried externally, but there was also a specialised bomber version, a single-seater with internal stowage. In place of the rear cockpit was a compartment containing four 65-lb bombs.

Although most of the British bombs were designed at the Royal Laboratory, which formed part of the famous Woolwich Arsenal, work on bombs was also done at the Royal Aircraft Factory, Farnborough, where the B.E., F.E., R.E. and S.E. series of aeroplanes were designed. One Farnborough-designed bomb was officially called 'Bomb, H.E., R.A.F., 336 lb, Mk I, Heavy Case', but was popularly called the R.A.F. three-hundredweight bomb. H.E. signified high explosive, as distinct from incendiary or other class of bomb; R.A.F. stood not for Royal Air Force but for the establishment named; Mk, or Mark, was the official term used to denote progressive improvements, Mk VIII, for example, denoting the eighth version; Heavy Case was an indication of the amount of metal in the case, or shell, of the bomb.

Two types of aircraft were used to carry the 336-lb bomb, one of which, the Martinsyde Elephant, was a single-seater. The other was the two/three-seat R.E.7, originally designed, as the R denoted, for reconnaissance. As in the case of all the 'Factory' aircraft, the E meant 'experimental', but was retained even after the aircraft had entered service. It must be further explained that the B in B.E. stood not for bomber, but for 'Blériot', meaning that the aircraft was of the tractor type, as popularised by the French constructor Louis Blériot.

The most remarkable British single-engined bomber, or day bomber, as it was sometimes called, remains to be mentioned. This was, in fact, the most remarkable machine of its class produced during the entire 1914–18 war, for it set an entirely new standard of performance, in terms of speed, altitude and rate of climb.

The de Havilland D.H.9A was a development of the D.H.4 and D.H.9 and continued to serve the RAF well long after the Armistice of 1918.

This outstanding machine was a product of the Aircraft Manufacturing Co, or Airco, and that it was designed by Capt (later Sir) Geoffrey de Havilland was denoted by the initials in its designation D.H.4. First tested in the autumn of 1916 with an engine of relatively low power, the D.H.4 achieved its highest performance, and its greatest fame, with the Rolls-Royce Eagle. With this engine a speed of just over 133 mph was attained at 10,000 ft, the time taken to climb to that height being nine minutes. This performance was somewhat reduced when bombs were carried, not only because of the weight of the bombs, but because they were hung externally beneath the wings and fuselage, and thus created drag.

The D.H.4 bore an amazingly close relationship to the de Havilland Mosquito of the Second World War, being faster than most fighters of the period, constructed of wood, having a Rolls-Royce power-plant and being manned by a crew of two. Unlike the Mosquito, however, it carried defensive armament, the pilot having a fixed Vickers gun and the observer/gunner one, or sometimes two, Lewis guns on a Scarff ring-mounting. Thus armed the D.H.4 could give a good account of itself in combat, for it was highly manoeuvrable. Of an attack by six of these bombers on Valenciennes in April 1917 it was officially recorded: 'A feature of their attack was the ease with which the de Havillands out-manoeuvred and outdistanced enemy fighters which endeavoured to intercept them.'

This superb bomber had one serious shortcoming: the two crew members were widely separated, and this made communication difficult in combat. On the next development, the D.H.9, the fault was rectified. Unhappily, it was necessary to fit an engine of lower power than the Eagle and performance suffered badly. The new engine was of B.H.P. or Siddeley Puma six-cylinder inline type and failures were frequent. On one occasion of 29 D.H.9s which set out on a raid fifteen had to return because of engine trouble. The next development, however, was a bomber in the true D.H.4 tradition which became famous in its own right.

The new bomber was slightly larger than the D.H.9 and was generally fitted with the equally new American Liberty twelve-cylinder water-cooled engine of 400 hp. Although troubles were at first experienced with the Liberty the D.H.9A, as the new type was called, soon established itself as an outstanding aircraft and remained in RAF service throughout the 1920s. Latterly, however, it was classed as a general purpose aircraft, and in addition to bombs was adapted to carry, as it was said, 'everything except the kitchen sink', especially for operation over desert areas.

	Span	Length	Crew	Loaded weight	Maximum speed	Armament
FRANCE						
Voisin X	58′ 10″	34′ 0″	2	4,850 lb	84 mph	1 c or 1 r-c m-g
Breguet-Michelin BM V	57′ 8″	26′ 1″	2	4,740 lb	86 mph	1 r-c m-g
Breguet 14 B2	49′ 0″	29′ 1″	2	4,145 lb	112 mph	2 r-c m-g
GERMANY						
L.V.G. C II	42′ 2″	26′ 7″	2	3,090 lb	85 mph	2 r-c m-g
GREAT BRITAIN						
F.E.2b	47′ 9″	32′ 2″	2	3,037 lb	91 mph	2 r-c m-g
D.H.4	42′ 5″	30′ 8″	2	3,472 lb	143 mph	2–3 r-c m-g
D.H.9A	45′ 11″	30′ 3″	2	4,645 lb	135 mph	2 r-c m-g

5

The 1920s and 1930s: Great Britain, France, Germany

Although the D.H.9A ranks as a de Havilland design, the task of adapting it from the D.H.9 was undertaken not by Airco but by the Westland company, the reason being that Airco was at the time fully occupied with the design of a new twin-engined bomber. This bomber, the D.H.10, was one of two such aircraft in production for the RAF at the Armistice. It was of striking appearance, for the fuselage was below the wings. Performance was of a high order, the top speed being about 126 mph, and at one stage consideration was given to using the type as a fighter. After the Armistice D.H.10s were used for air mail services between England and Germany and Cairo and Baghdad.

The second type of twin-engined bomber just mentioned, the Vickers Vimy, was also used as a mail-carrier in the Middle East: but it achieved a far greater distinction when, on 14/15 June 1919, flown by Alcock and Brown, it became the first aeroplane to make a nonstop Atlantic crossing. Like the D.H.10, the Vimy in its standard form was powered by two Rolls-Royce Eagle engines. The maximum bomb load was about 3,000 lb, and with this load the range was 550 miles, with the aircraft cruising at a speed of 90 mph at a height of 6,000 ft. With a light bomb load the range was 1,500 miles, and with extra petrol tanks the Transatlantic Vimy had a range of 2,440 miles. This Vimy is now exhibited in the Science Museum at South Kensington, London.

In post-war years the Vimy was adapted for training airmen in the use of parachutes. A small platform was built on each bottom wing, the occupant facing rearwards and holding the outermost and rearmost interplane bracing strut. Up in the air, and on a signal from the pilot, the trainee moved round behind the strut, and once he had released his parachute he was too late to change his mind about leaving the Vimy, for the canopy caught the air stream and hauled him off very smartly indeed.

The next Vickers bomber supplied to the RAF somewhat resembled the Vimy but was considerably larger. This was the Virginia, or 'Jinnie' to the men who flew and maintained the type between 1924 and 1937. Over the years the Virginia was extensively modified, notably in respect of defence against attacks by fighters from the rear. The first versions had a ventral, or belly, gun, firing from the bottom of the fuselage; then experiments were made with fighting tops, or gun positions perched on the top wing. Finally a gunner was installed behind the tail, as on the Handley Page V/1500.

Three types of Handley Page biplane bombers succeeded the V/1500 and O/400 in RAF service. These were the Hyderabad, Hinaidi and Heyford. The first-named types were identical in design, but whereas the Hyderabad had two Napier Lion water-cooled engines and was of wooden construction the Hinaidi had a metal structure and two Bristol Jupiter air-cooled radial engines. The radial engine, the cylinders of which diverged outward round a central crankcase, was widely used in bombers between the wars. Like the Virginia, the Hyderabad and Hinaidi carried their bombs externally, but in the Heyford the principal bombs were stowed in the specially thickened centre portion of the lower wing. This wing was some way below the fuselage and the upper wing was attached to the top of the fuselage. The two upper gunners thus had clear fields of fire for their Lewis guns. A third Lewis gun was installed in a retractable turret, or one which could be drawn up into the fuselage when not in use. This was also rotatable, and being cylindrical in form was quickly named the 'dustbin'. Heyfords were in squadron service between 1933 and 1939. A companion type, though not as widely used, was the Fairey Hendon, a monoplane having a wing of great thickness, wherein the bombs were carried. The undercarriage did not retract but was streamlined by massive trouser-like fairings, or casings.

All the aircraft just described were classed as night bombers and were twin-engined; but the RAF also took into service a small number of big single-

There were many different versions of the Vickers Virginia, but all bombers of the type used by RAF squadrons had two Napier Lion engines.

engined bombers which were suitable for night operation. The type concerned was the Avro Aldershot which, in 1924, when it came into use, was one of the largest single-engined aircraft in the world, having a wing span of nearly 70 ft. Also in service at the period was the Fairey Fawn single-engined two-seat day bomber which, partly by reason of the strict terms of the official specification to which it was designed, was appreciably slower than the wartime D.H.9A. This state of affairs was unacceptable to Mr C. R. (later Sir Richard) Fairey, who made up his mind to build a bomber to meet similar requirements but having a far higher speed. This was entirely a private venture, made without a promise of, though in hope of, a production order, and the story of the Fox, as the new bomber was named, is one of courage and romance.

In 1923 Fairey had seen an American Curtiss seaplane win the Schneider Trophy at a speed of over 177 mph. He was deeply impressed, and obtained from the American company the right to use certain features which had made the speed possible. First among these was the Curtiss D.12 engine, with its very low frontal area, or small

The Fairey Fox was the fastest bomber of its time and one of the most beautiful biplanes ever built.

cross-section, and consequently low drag. Next was the Curtiss-Reed metal propeller; third, the Curtiss surface radiators, made of corrugated brass sheet and forming part of the wing surfaces. In order to save drag still further the Fairey company developed its patented 'High-Speed' gun mounting, which, to-

gether with the Lewis gun it carried, folded down into the fuselage when not in use.

The Fox materialised as a single-bay biplane of great beauty, and in spite of early engine-cooling troubles the Fairey test pilot, Capt Norman Macmillan, was able to assure Fairey that he had 'a winner'. Eventually a demonstration was arranged for Air Chief Marshal Sir Hugh Trenchard, then Chief of the Air Staff, and remembered today as the 'father of the RAF'. After the demonstration the CAS took Macmillan aside and asked him frankly what he thought of the Fox. Did he, for instance, consider that it could be flown by young and comparatively inexperienced pilots? The test pilot wrote some years ago: 'I told him frankly that it was one of the easiest and most viceless aeroplanes I had ever flown. We walked back, and Sir Hugh Trenchard looked at Dick Fairey and said in his booming bass voice: "Mr Fairey, I have decided to order a squadron of Foxes." ' That squadron, No. 12, was the only one to be equipped with Foxes, but it became the pride of the RAF. A fox's head continued to be used as the squadron emblem until the unit, then equipped with four-jet Avro Vulcans, was disbanded in 1967.

Britain's Air Ministry now determined to follow the pattern set by the Fox, and in the late 1930s organised a competition for a new type of day bomber, or light bomber, to replace it. Fairey was not invited to submit an entry, but protested when he heard of the omission, and eventually a metal-built development of the original wooden Fox was matched against the Hawker Hart and Avro Antelope. There was little to choose between the three aircraft in terms of performance, but the Hart embodied a new system of metal construction which made it very easy to maintain in operational condition and contracts were duly awarded. The Hawker success was deserved for another reason: since 1926 the company had been supplying to the RAF a fine single-engined bomber powered, like the Avro Aldershot, with the Rolls-Royce Condor engine. As already mentioned, this engine had not been ready in time for the Handley Page V/1500. The Hawker Horsley was smaller than the Aldershot, but much larger than the Fox, though nearly 30 mph slower. It was an excellent aircraft especially in regard to load-carrying, and a special version broke the world's long-distance record by flying 3,420 miles in $34\frac{1}{2}$ hours, before coming down in the Persian Gulf. This record was never homologated, or officially registered by the Fédération Aéronautique Internationale, because two hours after it was established Lindbergh's flight across the Atlantic had succeeded it.

The Condor engine was not altogether successful and the Hart was fitted with the new and smaller Rolls-Royce Kestrel, likewise of twelve-cylinder water-cooled type. This was the British company's reply to the Curtiss D.12 and had been earlier installed in the Foxes of No. 12 Squadron in place of the original American engines. The same Rolls-

The Hawker Hart succeeded the Fairey Fox. On these Harts the large numerals denote the
number of the squadron. The smaller figures show the Service number.

Royce engine was installed in the metal Fox, or
Fox II, and, although no orders for this excellent
bomber were forthcoming from the RAF, it was
adopted by, and built in, Belgium.

The Kestrel proved to be an exceptionally fine
engine, and was installed not only in the Hart, but in

numerous derivative types, or aircraft developed
from it for other purposes. These included the
Demon and Osprey mentioned in *The World's
Fighters*. The only specialised bomber development
was the Hind, which had a more powerful version
of the Kestrel and, more important, one which

maintained its power at a greater height by means of a supercharger. This mechanical device supplied the engine with a greater weight of charge, or petrol/air mixture, than would have otherwise been possible at high altitudes, where the air was thin. The air being thin, drag was less, and, for a given power, the speed attainable was greater. After the Hind all RAF bombers had supercharged engines.

Among the types derived from the Hart was the Hardy, officially classed as a general purpose aircraft and specially equipped for service overseas. As already noted, this class of machine had really begun with the D.H.9A, and the RAF's GP types were essentially day bombers with special equipment. These types, in order of entry into service, were the Fairey IIIF; a direct D.H.9A replacement, the Westland Wapiti; the Fairey Gordon (a Fairey IIIF with Armstrong Siddeley Panther air-cooled radial engine instead of a water-cooled Napier Lion); Westland Wallace (a development of the Wapiti); and the Hawker Hardy already mentioned. Like the specialised Hart and Hind day bombers, these types carried some 500 lb of bombs under the wings. The bombs were sighted from a prone position assumed by the bomb-aimer on the floor of the fuselage, as on the Hart and Hind; and likewise in common with the two Hawker bombers they had a Vickers machine-gun for the pilot and a Lewis machine-gun for the bomb-aimer/gunner.

The Hind was the last of the RAF's biplane bombers, and the last of such bombers to have a single engine, except for the Vickers Wellesley and Fairey Battle. The Battle is best dealt with in a later chapter, together with the twin-engined Armstrong Whitworth Whitley, Bristol Blenheim, Handley Page Hampden and Vickers Wellington, for all these bombers, though introduced into RAF service before 1939, were widely employed against the Germans in the war which followed. The Wellesley, on the other hand, was mainly confined to service against the Italians overseas, though it has a particular interest in the story of bomber development because of the remarkable system of geodetic construction which it introduced. This system was based on the use of curved criss-cross members in a sort of lattice work, and was used not only for the fuselage but for the wings also. The resulting structure was so light, and the Wellesley was able to lift such a heavy load, that during 1938 two specially prepared aircraft of this type gained the world's long-distance record by flying from Ismailia, Egypt, to Darwin, Australia. The distance of 7,162 miles was covered nonstop in just under 48 hours. As it was not considered advisable to break up the geodetic pattern in order to carry the bombs internally they were suspended in streamlined containers, or bomb nacelles, beneath the wing. On the record-breaking flight, of course, no guns or bombs were carried.

The Wellesley was originally designed as a private venture to meet a specification for a general purpose aircraft, but when it entered service it was officially classed as a bomber. The distinctions made in the RAF between the so-called light or day bombers and the heavier twin-engined night bombers were now fast disappearing. Classification had, in any case, become somewhat confusing because not all their day bombers were of light single-engined type. The only exceptions, however, were the Boulton Paul Sidestrand, taken into service in 1928, and the later Overstrand; and the Overstrand was not truly a new design but merely a much improved Sidestrand. Moreover, only a single squadron was equipped with these bombers, though they were of unusual interest, apart from having strange-sounding names, borrowed from villages in Norfolk, where the Boulton Paul works were located.

The Sidestrand and Overstrand were descended from a remarkable twin-engined bomber named the Bourges, built by the Norfolk company in 1918. The most outstanding characteristic of the Bourges was its fighter-like manoeuvrability, and this was inherited in a marked degree by the later types. The effectiveness of the Sidestrand in combat was increased by its three gun positions: nose; mid-upper, or dorsal; and ventral. Historians have consistently credited the Sidestrand with having three guns, but this is incorrect, for there was one gun for either of the two last-named positions, depending on the position of a particular aircraft in a formation. Like bombers operating in daylight in the 1914–18 war, the crews of the Sidestrands were trained in formation flying to give each other covering fire: that is, to cover, or open fire over, areas screened by each others' blind spots, or areas over which shooting was impossible. The reasons why shooting was impossible were that parts of the aircraft got in the way and that the gun mountings themselves allowed only restricted fields of fire because of the difficulty in operating hand-held guns at the speeds then being attained. The Sidestrand's top speed was about 140 mph.

It was this last difficulty which led Boulton Paul to install in the Overstrand an enclosed power-driven turret, which reduced the gunner's physical task to that of operating a handle in the direction in which he wished the gun to point. This turret was perched out in the extreme nose of the Overstrand, and being cylindrical in form, caused the RAF's new bomber to become irreverently dubbed the Bandstand.

Overstrands equipped only one RAF squadron,

A power-driven gun turret was the most notable feature of the ▶ Boulton Paul Overstrand. Bombs were carried internally and externally.

but more extensive use of power-operated gun turrets was made on a Handley Page twin-engined monoplane bomber hastily developed from a transport aircraft to meet the demands of the RAF Expansion Scheme of the mid-1930s. The new type was named Harrow and was the last RAF bomber to have a non-retractable undercarriage. Retraction would have been very difficult because of the high-wing layout. By the time war came the Harrows had been replaced by Wellingtons, and were used only for second-line duties, such as transport. Transport Harrows were sometimes called Sparrows.

The development of bombers in France between the wars was generally along the same lines as in England, and the first of the French types was the Farman Goliath, already briefly mentioned. The first impression made by a Goliath was that its long-span wings, and for that matter its fuselage also, appeared to have been cut off by the yard; this impression was heightened by distinctive angular trousers to which the undercarriage wheels were attached. But this was an efficient bomber, even with the relatively low-powered 260 hp Salmson engines originally installed. The Farman type-number for the Goliath was F.60, and the F.60 M benefited from having 310 hp Renault engines. Then, in 1925, came a version with 380 hp Jupiter engines, of the type designed by the Bristol company

in England. There were other versions, including the F.68, supplied to Poland; but during 1928 what amounted to a new branch of the Goliath family began with the F.160. This had strengthened wings and more powerful engines and could carry 3,300 lb of bombs.

The four-engined Super Goliath biplane never entered squadron service, but in 1934 a very large four-engined seven-seater Farman bomber monoplane, the F.221, was put into production for the French Air Force. This was of high-wing type, the massive strut-braced wing being attached to the top of the fuselage; but the most striking feature was the mounting of tandem pairs of engines (as on the Handley Page V/1500) well below the wing. On the improved F.222, which was also placed in production, advantage was taken of this location of the engines, and of the nacelle they shared, to retract each mainwheel of the undercarriage into one of the nacelles.

The final bomber version was the F.2233, with new wing and tail and with Hispano-Suiza water-cooled engines instead of the Gnome-Rhône air-cooled radials previously fitted. In June 1940 the first two aircraft of this type operated, together with F.222s, against targets in Germany; but for the French Air Force as then constituted the war was nearly over.

And yet the story of the Farman bombers remains to be concluded, for on the night of 7/8 June 1940 an aircraft of generally similar type, bearing the type number F.2234, originally intended as a mail-carrier, later handed over to the French Aéronavale for maritime reconnaissance, and then adapted as a bomber, became the first Allied aircraft to bomb Berlin in the Second World War. The name of this aircraft was *Jules Verne*.

French bomber-builders between the wars, other than Farman, were Breguet, Lioré et Olivier, Amiot, Blériot, Bloch and Potez. The Breguet 19 biplane, which first appeared in 1921 and remained in service for over fifteen years, was produced as a specialised bomber (B2) but could fairly be classed together with Britain's general purpose types. This single-engined Breguet was a successor to the Type 14, and was of notably clean, or uncluttered, design; thus, there was only one interplane strut on each side, instead of four as on the Breguet 14, and the undercarriage likewise had only two struts, or legs. Bomb-carrying Breguets of the twin-engined monoplane 690 series were used against the Germans in 1940, but would be best considered as attack aircraft, or tactical bombers.

The Lioré et Olivier bomber series was initiated by the LeO 7/2, which, like its successor the LeO 12, was little used. Far more successful was the LeO 20 which somewhat resembled the Farman Goliath and which served the French Air Force for many years as a night bomber, until being finally withdrawn from squadrons during 1937. In January of that year the same manufacturers flew the prototype of a twin-engined monoplane bomber which contrasted as sharply as it possibly could have done with the LeO 20. This was the LeO 45, one of the most elegant aeroplanes of its time. Notwithstanding the fact that the intended engines were not forthcoming, and that a compromise had to be made in respect of propellers, a speed of over 300 mph was attained. One possible bomb load was two bombs of 1,100 lb and five of 440 lb, internally stowed, and with the load reduced to 1,100 lb the range was 1,430 miles. Defensive armament was a fixed rifle-calibre machine-gun in the nose, which must have been of very limited use, although the aircraft could perform fighter-like aerobatic manoeuvres after dropping its bombs; a similar gun in a retractable ventral turret; and a 20-mm cannon in a retractable power-operated dorsal turret.

In appearance and performance the graceful LeO 45, the production version of which was the LeO 451, seemed to make amends for a number of French bombers which had preceded it; and among the less elegant of these were the Amiot 122 and 143. Both were marked not only by unattractiveness of line but by diversity of purpose, and in the instance of the former type this diversity was signified by the suffix BP 3. The meaning of this was that the aircraft was a three-seater for 'bombardement protection', that is a bomber capable of escorting and defending other, larger, bombers. A single-engined biplane, the Amiot 122 BP 3 had a fuselage of such plumpness that it acquired the nickname of la Grosse Julie, or Fat Julie.

The twin-engined Amiot 143 of 1934 was not so much plump as angular. As related in *The World's Fighters*, the French at one time carried on a flirtation with a class of aircraft described as multiplace de combat, or multi-seat battleplane; but although fighting was, in theory at least, among their duties, they were essentially bombers. There were nose, dorsal and ventral gun positions, the last-named being at the rear of an under-structure which might fairly be compared with the Hanging Gardens of Babylon.

The Amiot 143 is best remembered not for its appearance but for its determined leaflet-dropping and bombing raids on Germany. Yet Amiot were determined also to attone for their earlier ugly aeroplanes, for their 350 series of bombers (Types 351–354), the first production orders for which were placed in 1938, rivalled in elegance and performance the LeO 45. One basic difference was that,

whereas the fuselage of the LeO 45 was of deep, narrow, oval cross-section, that of the Amiot was of circular section.

A prototype of the Amiot 350, designated 340-01, was involved in a flight of more than usual interest in the summer of 1938. The French Chief of Air Staff had been invited to visit Germany, and the chosen vehicle was this prototype, somewhat doctored to give the appearance that the new Amiot bomber was already in service. German Intelligence would certainly have been premature in assuming this.

A French bomber which shared the angularity of the Amiot 143 was the somewhat earlier Blériot 127/2, descended from a large escort fighter. The monoplane wing was of such thickness that a man could pass from the fuselage to each engine nacelle in flight. There was some purpose in this, for although he could do little for an ailing engine, there was a machine-gun position in the tail of each nacelle.

Two twin-engined monoplane bombers in service with French squadrons during the late 1930s were the wood-and-metal Potez 540 and the all-metal Bloch 200. Whereas the main undercarriage wheels of the Potez bomber retracted into the engine nacelles, which were hung under the wing as on the four-engined Farmans mentioned earlier, the Bloch machine had a non-retractable undercarriage. This

Among the French bombers which were not things of beauty was the Amiot 143, as this picture
bears witness. Later Amiots and Lioré et Oliviers displayed great purity of form.

was one feature which contributed to a poor performance, and a low-wing development with retractable undercarriage, the Bloch 210, had a top speed
of over 180 mph, whereas the Bloch 200 could hardly
exceed 140 mph. More refined twin-engined low-
wing Bloch bombers which entered service were the
Types 131 and 175. Of these the second was the more
successful, and having tested specimens the Germans
kept the type in production, ordering that no arma-

ment should be installed; but although the Bloch 175
had a top speed of about 320 mph the Germans
decided to use the power eggs, or the complete,
self-contained engine/airscrew/cowling installations,
in their enormous Messerschmitt Me 323 transports.

By the time war came in 1939 the Germans themselves had considerable recent experience in the
construction and operation of bombers, for, in
defiance of the Treaty of Versailles (1919) they had

begun secretly during the 1920s to establish a new air force. In the mid-1930s this emerged openly as the Luftwaffe (Air Weapon), and the first large bomber to be taken into service was an adaptation of the Junkers-Ju 52/3m transport aeroplane, which has a place of honour in the companion volume *The World's Airliners*. The significance of the designation 3m was that three engines were fitted. This arrangement was not generally favoured for bombers because the presence of an engine in the nose of the fuselage made it impossible for the bomb-aimer to take his station there, and, even if the bombs were aimed from a position close behind the engine, noise and vibration could prove distracting. Thus the Ju 52/3m was regarded by the Germans as an interim type, or one that had to serve until something better became available. Nevertheless, bombers of this type saw service in the Spanish Civil War. A feature was a dustbin gun-turret, somewhat similar to that on the Handley Page Heyford. A number of smaller single-engined Junkers-W 34s were also used by the Germans as bombers, but a more important type was the Ju 86.

Like the more famous Heinkel He 111 the twin-engined Ju 86 made its first appearance as an airliner. A bomber version quickly came on the scene, and this was another German military aeroplane which first saw action in the Spanish Civil War.

The early Ju 86 bombers were not especially notable aeroplanes, but later developments, to be described in another chapter, proved very remarkable indeed.

To the names of Junkers and Heinkel must now be added one hardly less famous in bomber history, and this by reason of the fact that in about 1930 the Dornier company in Switzerland were testing a 'mail- and freight-carrier' called the Do F. This was soon developed into a bomber, and entered production in Germany as the Do 13. An improved, and more common, version was the Do 23, a high-wing twin-engined monoplane like its predecessor, and similarly having a non-retractable undercarriage. The table of data indicates that performance was not spectacular. The figures are, nevertheless, significant, for a quick scanning of the column headed 'maximum speed' indicates that during the 1920s and 1930s the speed of bombers was roughly trebled, the Do 23 representing the half-way stage both in time and speed.

It must not be inferred from the table however that on the coming of war in 1939 the only bombers having speeds of the 250–300 mph order were French. The Amiot 350 and LeO 45 series of bombers have, in fact, been included in the present chapter for two particular reasons: first, they were little used as bombers in the war; secondly, they afford a very striking indication of technical advance in two decades. When war came fast bombers were also available to Britain and Germany; but as they achieved their fame as bombers of the Second World War their origins and development are best described later. Especially notable among these aircraft were the British Bristol Blenheim and the German Dornier Do 17.

	Span	Length	Crew	Loaded weight	Maximum speed	Service ceiling	Armament
GREAT BRITAIN							
Vickers Vimy	67′ 2″	43′ 6″	3	12,500 lb	103 mph	7,000 ft	3–4 r-c m-g
Vickers Virginia X	87′ 8″	62′ 3″	4	17,600 lb	108 mph	10,000 ft	3–4 r-c m-g
Handley Page Hyderabad	75′ 0″	59′ 2″	4	13,590 lb	109 mph	14,000 ft	3 r-c m-g
Handley Page Heyford	75′ 0″	58′ 0″	3	16,750 lb	142 mph	20,000 ft	3 r-c m-g
Fairey Fox	38′ 0″	31′ 2″	2	4,117 lb	153 mph	17,000 ft	2 r-c m-g
Hawker Hart	37′ 3″	29′ 4″	2	4,554 lb	175 mph	21,300 ft	2 r-c m-g
Boulton Paul Sidestrand	71′ 11″	46′ 0″	3	10,200 lb	140 mph	24,000 ft	2 r-c m-g
FRANCE							
Farman Goliath	86′ 11″	47′ 7″	2–3	12,785 lb	90 mph	18,000 ft	2 r-c m-g
Farman F.222	118′ 1″	70′ 9″	5	41,225 lb	199 mph	19,700 ft	3–5 r-c m-g
Breguet 19	48′ 8″	31′ 3″	2	4,850 lb	141 mph	22,000 ft	2 r-c m-g
Amiot 143	80′ 2″	58′ 11″	4	21,000 lb	190 mph	26,000 ft	4 r-c m-g
Amiot 354	74′ 11″	47′ 7″	4	24,910 lb	298 mph	31,000 ft	1 c+2 r-c m-g
Lioré et Olivier LeO 451	73′ 11″	56′ 4″	4	25,130 lb	307 mph	29,530 ft	1 c+2 r-c m-g
GERMANY							
Junkers-Ju 52/3m	95′ 10″	62′ 0″	3–4	24,200 lb	165 mph	16,600 ft	2 r-c m-g
Junkers-Ju 86	73′ 10″	57′ 9″	4	18,080 lb	202 mph	22,300 ft	3 r-c m-g
Dornier Do 23	84′ 0″	61′ 8″	4	20,280 lb	161 mph	13,750 ft	3 r-c m-g

6

The 1920s and 1930s: USA, USSR, Italy, Japan

Of the three names chiefly associated with American bombers in the years immediately following the 1914–18 war, one, that of Martin, is still familiar. The other two, Huff-Daland and Keystone, are now only distantly remembered.

Young Glenn Martin built his first aeroplane in 1912, and after a partnership with the Wright company set up his own business in 1917. Early in 1918 this company was awarded a contract to build ten twin-engined bombers, known as MB-1s. Although the order was a small one the bombers were quite large, slightly larger in fact than the Vickers Vimy. Two Liberty engines were fitted and armament was disposed as on the Vimy. The somewhat

larger MB-2 was built in bigger numbers, but only twenty came from the Martin factory, the greater quantities being ordered from other makers, including Curtiss. These bombers were officially known by the designation NBS-1, the letters signifying night bomber, short-range, and numbered among them were twenty having turbo-superchargers, driven on the waterwheel principle by the exhaust gases. This type of supercharger was to become a standard fitting on American bombers of the Second World War.

In the late 1920s America followed the lead of Britain and France by taking into service a type of large single-engined bomber. This was built by the

Huff-Daland company and was known as the LB-1, the letters standing for light bomber. By the time deliveries began in 1927, however, large single-engined bombers had fallen into disfavour in America and Huff-Daland produced a twin-engined version which entered service as the LB-5. The LB-5A was distinguished not only in having twin fins and rudders for directional stability and control, instead of one assembly as on its predecessor, but in bearing the name Keystone instead of Huff-Daland. This was because the earlier company was reorganised in 1927 as the Keystone Aircraft Corporation. With various changes in design, and in the type of engine fitted, Keystone bombers entered service with the designations LB-6, LB-7, B-3A, B-4A, B-5A and B-6A, and with the dropping of the L from the last-named series the long succession of American B (bombardment) aircraft began. This continues today with the B-58 Hustler.

With their biplane wings and fixed undercarriages the Keystone bombers had at best a top speed of only about 120 mph. Progress in the design of large bombers seemed, in fact, to have stagnated; then, in 1931 the Boeing company showed what could be achieved by a twin-engined bomber having a monoplane wing, a smooth metal skin instead of fabric covering, and a retractable undercarriage. To be scrupulously accurate the undercarriage of the

Boeing YB-9, as the new bomber was known, was semi-retractable, a portion of each mainwheel being left exposed. A similar feature was observed on a Martin twin-engined bomber tested in 1932, and which was ordered into production as the B-10. This was the first monoplane bomber to be built in large numbers, and with its speed of over 200 mph it could truly be described as revolutionary, for it was capable of outstripping contemporary fighters. Not only were the bombs carried internally but the crew of three had enclosed cockpits, and such was the performance and popularity of the type that it was soon ordered by other air forces, notably that of the Netherlands East Indies. The later aircraft in the Netherlands contract were especially striking in appearance, for a continuous transparent 'greenhouse' enclosure ran along most of the top of the fuselage between the pilot's and the rear-gunner's cockpits.

The company founded by Glenn Martin was not, however, to have things all its own way in the bomber business. The first Martin bomber had, in fact, been designed not by Mr Martin but by another young man named Donald Douglas who, in 1920, established the company which bears his name with the highest distinction to this day. When, during the mid-1930s, a replacement was needed for the Martin B-10, the Douglas company designed a special

During the 1920s and 1930s the Martin company was in the forefront of bomber development.
The B-10 seen here was its most outstanding achievement.

bomber-type fuselage which could be used with the wings and other parts of the famous DC-2 transport, then in production. The result was the B-18, a fine aeroplane but one which was inevitably over-shadowed by the historic Boeing B-17, or Flying Fortress. The later B-23 development of the B-18 had a smaller fuselage.

To be strictly accurate the B-18 was not the first Douglas bomber to be used by the US Army Air Force, for in 1930 the company had been awarded a Service test contract for seven YB-7s; Service test meaning that, though not built in large numbers,

the type concerned was interesting enough to be tested under operational conditions, this being signified by the prefixed letter Y. The most remarkable feature of the YB-7, which was about 60 mph faster than the Keystone bombers then equipping the American squadrons, was its gull wing, or one the inner sections of which sloped down to join the top of the fuselage independently. This feature improved the field of view and the fields of fire for the defensive machine-guns.

It is not always appreciated that the world-famous four-engined B-17 was designed to the same specification, or set of official requirements, as the twin-engined B-18. This specification laid down that the new bomber should be multi-engined and Boeing chose to interpret multi as 'four'.

The first Flying Fortress, as the B-17 was called, differed considerably from the later aircraft of the name, especially respecting armament. In this regard the name was hardly appropriate, for the original complement of five machine-guns, three of which were installed in transparent blisters on the sides and bottom of the fuselage, proved seriously inadequate. However, the first bomber of the type, then bearing the maker's designation Model 299, quickly gave notice of its performance capabilities by flying across the American continent at an average speed of 252 mph. No bomber before it had achieved a speed of this order. The story of what followed this historic flight is best told later.

The only type of military aircraft built in the USA and used in action during the 1914–18 war was the de Havilland D.H.4, and bombers of this type, including versions with the cockpits placed next to each other as on the D.H.9 and 9A, continued in service after 1918. The USSR used another improved version of the D.H.9A, thus further testifying to the excellence of the original D.H.4 of 1916, for on this basic type all these later developments were based.

After the R-1, as the Soviet development of the D.H.9A was called, two-seat single-engined bombers of indigenous origin, that is, designed entirely in the Soviet Union, were taken into use, serving also, as had the R-1, for reconnaissance. These were the Tupolev R-3 and Polikarpov R-5. The R-3 was especially interesting by reason of its all-metal construction, using a Russian-developed aluminium alloy, claimed to be stronger than the duralumin then (1926 onwards) becoming fairly common in other countries. A pioneer of duralumin construction was the German Junkers company, and it is not, perhaps, widely known that three-engined Junkers bombers, designated R-42, were taken into service by the Russians in 1925/26 to replace Farman Goliaths. A feature of these bombers was a retractable dustbin turret.

The form of construction used in the Tupolev R-3 was also used in the twin-engined TB-1, bearing the same famous designer's name. A leading part in the design, however, was played by V. M. Petlyakov, a man whose name will reappear in connection with later types of Soviet bombers. The TB-1 proved to have a good performance, especially respecting range; but although it had a thick monoplane wing the undercarriage was not retractable and the top speed was little more than 120 mph.

The far larger four-engined TB-3 will be remem-

The Tupolev TB-3, or ANT-6, was used in large numbers during the 1920s and 1930s. It was employed
for the dropping of parachutists as well as for bombing.

bered by cinema-goers between the wars because of its rather frightening appearance, with its vast wing and stilty four-wheeled main undercarriage, between the legs of which it sometimes carried a tank (of the armoured, crawling type). TB-3s were also used in experiments with parasite fighters, these being carried above the wing for launching in the event of attack – a method of defence which never became popular. Many alterations were made in design, and by 1937 the corrugated, or furrowed, metal skin was being replaced by a smooth skin. Late-model TB-3s were in service when the USSR entered the war, and an example captured by the Germans was found to have provision for 12,800 lb

of bombs. This was only for a short range, however, and a more normal load was 4,400 lb. Like certain other types of obsolete, or out-dated, bombers, TB-3s continued for a long period in service as transports.

On the Ilyushin DB-3, the last type of Soviet bomber to be considered for the present, there was no stilty undercarriage hanging down and creating drag. Instead the mainwheels were semi-retractable, as on the more-or-less contemporary (1935) American bombers. The DB-3, again like the Martins, was a compact twin-engined design. Maximum bomb load was nearly 5,000 lb, but less than half this load was normal.

It has been shown that the Italians were early in the field of big-bomber development and that some of their types were of striking appearance and good performance. Development continued along quite individual lines between the wars, and although nothing quite as spectacular as the Caproni triplanes was ever again seen in Italian squadrons, from the mid-1920s well into the 1930s Caproni were building bombers of very striking appearance. These were of inverted sesquiplane layout: that is, they were one-and-a-half-wingers though with the smaller wing carried above the larger one, in reversal of the usual practice. Readers of *The World's Fighters* may recall that the Fiat company used a similar arrangement for its C.R.1 single-seater. With various refinements the Ca 73, the first of the curious new Capronis to enter service, was developed as the Ca 73bis (second), Ca 73ter (third), later called Ca 82, Ca 88 and Ca 89. In all these variants the two Isotta-Fraschini or Lorraine water-cooled engines were carried in a nacelle, or power egg, between the wings, one driving a tractor and one a pusher propeller. As the fuselage was small in cross-section, or frontal area, the bombs were carried externally.

Caproni next turned to the high-wing monoplane layout for a series of bombers (Ca 101, Ca 111, Ca 133) which, having far more spacious fuselages, enabled them to be used alternatively as transports and ambulances in Italy's East African campaigns. These Capronis were really of the class which the French called type coloniale, a description which calls for no explanation.

Seeking higher speeds, Caproni turned to the mid-wing monoplane layout, which had been made popular by the Martin B-10 and enabled the bombs to be carried snugly inside, beneath the centre section of the wing, which ran through the fuselage. The Ca 135 was fast, having a top speed of over 270 mph, and, with its three heavy machine-guns, well armed.

When they adopted a low-wing arrangement for the Ca 309 and Ca 310 Caproni had tried most wing positions in the book; but these types were of relatively low performance, being intended for colonial operation and having less power than the specialised Ca 135. Nor did later, higher-powered, derivatives show a greatly superior performance.

The great Fiat concern entered the bomber business in 1918/1919 and tested during the latter year a single-engined two-seater called the B.R.1. This had the same zig-zag, or W, arrangement of bracing struts that Fiat adopted for their inter-war biplane fighters: the R in the designation acknowledged that the designer was in both instances Rosatelli. Developed versions were the B.R.2 and B.R.3, which were used well into the 1930s. In 1936, however, a Rosatelli bomber of vastly differing type appeared, and this was ready in time to be used in small numbers in the Spanish Civil War. This bomber was the B.R.20, a type which corresponded roughly with Germany's He 111 and Britain's Vickers Wellington, and which was the only Italian bomber to operate against the British Isles. As a former RAF intelligence officer, the present writer recalls examining a specimen shot down in Suffolk and discovering that the item of principal interest (apart from some excellent cheese and coffee) was a power-driven gun-turret, with a heavy machine-gun, in the dorsal position. Nevertheless, like the comparable German and British bombers named, the B.R.20 proved to be inadequately armed, and the later B.R.20bis had a gun not only in the nose, ventral and dorsal positions, but in each of two blisters on the fuselage sides.

The most distinctive feature of the Savoia Marchetti bombers, or the greater number of them, was their triple-engine installation, as on Germany's Ju 52. The Italian bombers differed, however, in being largely of wooden construction, and only the first to enter service, the S.M.81, had a fixed undercarriage, as on the German machine together with which it served in Spain. A more refined design was the S.M.79, developed, like the Ju 52 and S.M.81, from an airliner, though in this instance

from one having a retractable undercarriage. Consequently the S.M.79 was quite fast, with a top speed of over 260 mph, and further refinement of design resulted in the more elegant S.M.84. A twin-engined version of the S.M.79, the S.M.79B, was exported, but was never used by Italian squadrons. S.M.79s were serving as transports until 1952.

Savoia Marchetti were not alone in building three-engined bombers for the Italian Air Force, for in 1939 quantity production was ordered of the Cant Z. 1007 bis, a monoplane of very refined appearance and largely of wooden construction. One general criticism of this type of construction is that it may be affected by extremes of temperature, but the Z.1007bis rendered good service in Africa as well as Russia. A twin-engined development, the Z.1018, was of even more refined appearance, but few of these were in service by the time Italy surrendered in 1943.

With one very remarkable exception, to be mentioned later, Japanese bombers between the wars may conveniently be classified as single-engined and twin-engined, and further sub-classified under the headings of two manufacturers, Kawasaki and Mitsubishi. The Kawasaki types are quickly disposed of, being all single-engined types of no particular military significance, though not without technical interest. The first of these was the Type

Three-engined bombers were widely used by the Italians during the 1930s and 1940s. This is a
Savoia Marchetti S.M.79, photographed during the Second World War.

88-II biplane, the work of the famous German designer Dr Richard Vogt, which had rigid struts instead of the usual flying wires. Wires so described run upwards and outwards to prevent deflection of the wing by the lift forces acting upon it. The second was the Ki-3, which had more normal bracing and carried about twice the bomb load (1,100 lb). The third was the Ki-32 monoplane, which had a good performance for its day in spite of having a fixed undercarriage and which saw extensive service in the war against China.

A Mitsubishi bomber strictly comparable with the Ki-32, but having an air-cooled radial, instead of a liquid-cooled inline, engine was the Ki-30. Some years earlier this had been preceded in service by the 2MB1 biplane, used in Manchuria. The design of the relatively small Ki-2 twin-engined bomber was based on that of a Junkers K-37 which had been presented to the Japanese Army. There were two main versions of the Ki-2, the first with fixed undercarriage and open crew positions, the second with retractable undercarriage and cockpit enclosures. A larger Mitsubishi twin-engined bomber was the G3M, another type more or less contemporary with, and comparable with, the He 111 and Wellington. During the Sino–Japanese war which preceded the Japanese attack on Pearl Harbor in 1941, bombers of this type made spectacular (for the period) long-distance raids on Hangkow and Nanking, flying from airfields in Kyushu and Formosa. The G3M was a Naval type, though flown from shore bases, and was used in the historic attack on HMS *Repulse* and HMS *Prince of Wales* three days after the assault on Pearl Harbor.

The remarkable exception among Japanese bombers was remarkable indeed, although, like the Ki-2 and G3M, it was essentially of German Junkers design. The story of this aeroplane really began as early as 1928, when Mitsubishi bought the rights to build a bomber version of the immense Junkers-G 38. Although only six bombers of the type were built they merit notice here for two reasons: first, they actually entered service; second, they were the largest military aircraft to do so in the period now under study. The wing span of 'The Monster', as the type was known, was over 144 ft and the bomb load could be varied between 4,400 lb and 11,000 lb. Eight machine-guns and a cannon formed the defensive armament.

Although the G3M has rightly been compared with the He 111 and Wellington, an even closer comparison may be made between these types and the Mitsubishi Ki-21, the first deliveries of which were made in 1938. This type was developed for the Japanese Army and remained in service throughout the war. Like other bombers of its class it was found to be inadequately armed, and the number of rifle-calibre machine-guns installed was increased from three to five or six. One of these guns was mounted in the extreme tail, a type of installation which became known during the war as a stinger. In the final version a heavy machine-gun was installed in a dorsal turret; earlier models had a rifle-calibre gun mounted in a long transparent enclosure of the type commonly called a greenhouse.

Other countries producing bombers in the years between the wars were Belgium (as already noted in connection with the Fairey Fox), Czechoslovakia, the Netherlands, Poland, Rumania and Switzerland. The types concerned were mostly single-engined, but there were some interesting exceptions. Czechoslovakia, for instance, built a bomber version of the Dutch Fokker F.IX three-engined airliner, some examples of which had a retractable ventral gun turret. A remarkable instance of international involvement was the exporting of two of these Dutch-designed Czechoslovak-built bombers to Yugoslavia. These had British-designed Jupiter

Mitsubishi G3M bombers of the type seen here with bombs slung beneath the fuselage were used
by the Japanese in their attacks on HMS *Prince of Wales* and *Repulse*.

engines – built under licence in France!

The Dutch themselves used a version of the
Fokker F.VII/3m airliner and in later years a
specialised Fokker twin-engined bomber designated
T.V. Though unremarkable in a technical sense
T.Vs made some valiant attacks on German forces
after the invasion of May 1940. In particular they
are credited with destroying thirty German aircraft
on the airfield at Wallhaven, Rotterdam. A comparable Polish type was the P.Z.L. P.37, developed
to replace a bomber version of the Fokker F.VII/3m
as built in Poland. The P.37 was a more notable

technical achievement than the Fokker T.V, with which it shared the distinction of inflicting considerable casualties on the invading Germans. A number of P.37s were flown to Rumania and were used by the Rumanian Air Force against the Russians.

	Span	Length	Crew	Loaded weight	Maximum speed	Service ceiling	Armament
USA							
Martin MB-2	74′ 2″	42′ 8″	4	12,120 lb	99 mph	8,500 ft	3 r-c m-g
Keystone LB-6	75′ 0″	43′ 5″	4	13,440 lb	114 mph	11,650 ft	3 r-c m-g
Martin B-10	70′ 6″	44′ 9″	3	14,600 lb	213 mph	24,200 ft	3 r-c m-g
Douglas B-18	89′ 6″	57′ 10″	6	27,670 lb	215 mph	23,900 ft	3 r-c m-g
USSR							
Tupolev TB-1	89′ 11″	59′ 0″	6	15,040 lb	123 mph	15,400 ft	6 r-c m-g
Tupolev TB-3	132′ 10″	82′ 8″	6	41,000 lb	140 mph	15,100 ft	10 r-c m-g
Ilyushin DB-3	70′ 2″	46′ 11″	3	20,600 lb	240 mph	27,500 ft	3 r-c m-g
ITALY							
Caproni Ca 73	82′ 0″	49′ 6″	4	11,025 lb	109 mph	15,000 ft	3 r-c m-g
Caproni Ca 135	61′ 8″	47′ 2″	4	21,050 lb	273 mph	21,300 ft	3 h m-g
Fiat B.R.20	70′ 9″	54′ 9″	4	22,270 lb	273 mph	26,200 ft	1 h m-g+2 r-c m-g
Savoia Marchetti S.M.79	69′ 6″	51′ 10″	5	23,100 lb	267 mph	21,300 ft	3 h m-g+2 r-c m-g
Cant Z.1007bis	81′ 4″	61′ 0″	5	29,200 lb	280 mph	24,600 ft	2 h m-g+2 r-c m-g
JAPAN							
Mitsubishi G3M	82′ 0″	54′ 0″	5	16,850 lb	216 mph	24,500 ft	1 c+3 r-c m-g
Mitsubishi Ki-21	73′ 10″	52′ 6″	5	17,450 lb	268 mph	28,200 ft	6 r-c m-g

7

The Second World War:
Great Britain, USA, USSR

In an earlier chapter mention was made of five types of British bomber, the Armstrong Whitworth Whitley, Bristol Blenheim, Fairey Battle, Handley Page Hampden and Vickers Wellington, because these had entered service with the RAF just before war came in 1939. The Whitley was a twin-engined mid-wing monoplane, the first three versions of which had air-cooled Armstrong Siddeley Tiger engines, though the later marks had liquid-cooled Rolls-Royce Merlin engines of the outstandingly successful type which was to remain in service until after the war. Another difference between the earlier and later marks was in armament, the most significant change being the fitting in the Mk IV of a power-operated turret having no fewer than four Browning rifle-calibre machine-guns. This was by far the heaviest concentration of firepower on any bomber of the time and became a standard feature on British bombers which long outlived the Whitley in service. Whitleys dropped six million leaflets over Germany on the first night of the war and were the first RAF bombers to attack Italy.

Smaller and very much faster than the Whitley was the Bristol Blenheim, which had an unusual history, not unlike that of the Fairey Fox. In 1935 the Bristol company built for Lord Rothermere a monoplane of the class which would today be known as an executive, or business, aircraft. This achieved the then sensational speed of 280 mph and was presented by Lord Rothermere to the nation. Quickly a bomber version was developed from it. Every effort was made to keep the new bomber as clean as possible, that is to avoid drag-producing excrescences, or items jutting out; accordingly the single power-driven gun turret was made partly retractable into the fuselage. In the first Blenheims to go to the RAF the pilot and navigator/bomb-aimer sat together in the extreme front of the fuselage, which was of curious insect-like form, being made up of several flat transparent panels. In the original nose the work of navigation was not easy, so a new mark, the Mk IV, or long-nosed Blenheim, was taken into service. Even in this version the nose was curious, for to give the pilot the best possible field of view a trough or furrow was let into the roof of the navigation compartment on the port side. As the war progressed many changes were made, especially in armament, but these changes, including a gun in a blister under the nose reduced the speed considerably.

Armament proved to be grievously inadequate in the Fairey Battle, which had a single Merlin engine. This was the last of the RAF's single-engined bombers, and though having the same type of engine as the Spitfire and Hurricane fighters, was much slower because of its greater size and weight.

Squadrons of Battles went to France with the British Advanced Air Striking Force and the shortcomings of the type became sadly apparent on 30 September 1939. On that day four out of a formation of five Battles were shot down by German Messerschmitt Me 109 fighters. On 10 May 1940, Battles attacked the bridges over the River Meuse at Maastricht. The RAF's first Victoria Crosses of the war were awarded after that raid. These however were made posthumously, that is after death. Ten days later forty Battles out of a striking force of 71 failed to return.

The Battle was a good aeroplane but a poor fighting machine, too slow and underarmed; but many of the losses may be attributed to operation in daylight.

Between the Handley Page Hampden and Vickers Wellington there were very marked differences; and between the Hampden and previous bombers of the same make the differences were greater still. Whereas the earlier Harrow had pioneered the installation of a power-driven gun turret in the extreme tail, the Hampden had no turrets whatsoever. In the nose was a fixed gun for the pilot, a type of installation which had not been seen on a large British bomber since the Aldershot and Horsley and which proved almost useless in time of war. A second gun, having a limited arc of fire, was also

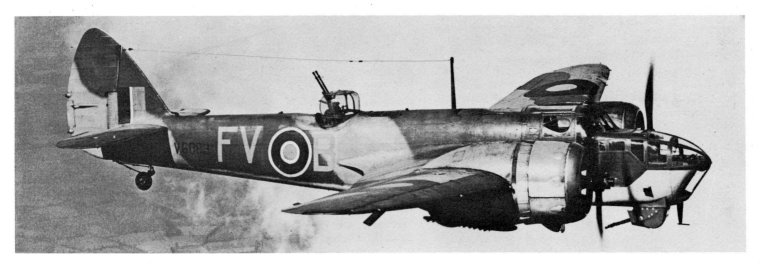

As first constructed the Bristol Blenheim was very 'clean' in appearance, but extra guns and other equipment, as seen, marred its purity of line.

fitted in the nose, and behind the wing were a dorsal and a ventral gun. In order that these should have a clear field of fire the rear fuselage was made very slender, and as the forward part was narrow and slab-sided the Hampden soon became known as the 'Flying Suitcase'. When war came the Hampden's rear armament proved gravely inadequate and was quickly doubled, and the type was later assigned solely to night operations, on which it continued until 1942.

Compared with the Hampden the Wellington looked very plump and had a power-driven gun turret in the nose and at the rear. With two guns in each turret it was considered to be adequately armed, especially as machines in a formation could give each other covering fire; but on 18 December 1939 ten Wellingtons of a force numbering 24 were shot down and three were badly damaged. Thereafter night operations became general. Ability to return to base after sustaining severe battle damage was one reason why the 'Wimpey' (so named after Popeye's hungry companion J. Wellington Wimpey) was popular among its crews. This ability was owed largely to the geodetic form of construction inherited by the Wellington from the Wellesley; but whereas the earlier type had carried its bombs in containers

The Handley Page Hampden was far more slender than the portly Wellington and was sometimes called the 'Flying Suitcase' because of its shape.

under the wing the Wellington carried them inside the fuselage. As the war proceeded, bigger and bigger bombs were developed for the RAF, and early in 1941 Wellingtons were beginning to deliver the 4,000-pounders which received the name blockbuster. Numerous versions of the Wellington were produced and during the early years of the war the type was the finest and most widely used of all the British bombers. Nearly 11,500 Wellingtons were built, but not all of these were bombers, some, for example, being used for over-water reconnaissance. A generally similar, but larger, aircraft called the Warwick was never used for bombing at all, although intended for the purpose.

During 1940 the RAF took into service the Short

Stirling, its first four-engined bomber since the Handley Page V/1500. It was an impressive aeroplane but was somewhat handicapped for a number of reasons. For instance, the Air Ministry insisted that the wing span should be short enough to allow it to be housed in standard hangars. This meant that in order to obtain the necessary wing area to lift the required load the aspect ratio of the wing, a term previously explained, was low. This resulted in a comparatively low service ceiling. Another disadvantage was that the bomb bay was divided into sections, which meant that the largest bomb that could be carried was a 4,000-pounder. The maximum bomb load was, in fact, 14,000 lb, and with this load the range was 590 miles. With the bomb load reduced

Vickers Wellington crew-members with one of their 'Wimpeys'. ▶

to 3,500 lb the range was about 2,000 miles.

Late in 1940 the Stirling was followed into service by another four-engined bomber, the Handley Page Halifax. This had originally been designed to have two engines only, these being of a new type known as the Rolls-Royce Vulture. The Vulture may be considered as two Merlins in one, the top one upright and the lower one inverted, so that seen end-on the engine was in the form of an X. When it seemed that there would be a shortage of Vultures the design of the airframe was altered to allow four ordinary Merlins to be fitted, and with these engines the Halifax Mk I entered service, as mentioned, in 1940. Alterations as the war progressed were numerous. For example, whereas the Mk I had two machine-guns in the nose turret, four in the tail turret and sometimes beam guns also (that is, firing outwards from the sides of the fuselage), the Mk II had no beam guns but a two-gun dorsal turret instead. Various measures were taken to reduce drag, including removal of the nose turret, which, in any case was little used as Halifaxes were generally operated at night and attacks in the forward hemisphere, or field of fire covered by the nose guns, were rare. Another alteration was an increase in the area of the fins, mounted at the tips of the horizontal tailplane to give directional stability, or cause the aircraft to fly in a straight line. This reduced the effects of yaw, or swing about the vertical axis, and consequently improved bombing accuracy. Well over 6,000 Halifaxes were built and one of these was the first RAF bomber to use the secret H2S blind bombing radar device. As suggested, this enabled the bomb-aimer to do his job without himself seeing the target.

Fine aeroplane though it was, the Halifax never achieved quite the success or fame of the Avro Lancaster, with which it was closely comparable; but even the Lancaster did not have a trouble-free birth. Mention has already been made of the Vulture engine, and it must now be recorded that late in 1940, the RAF took into service a new type of large twin-engined bomber called the Avro Manchester. The engines in this bomber were Vultures, but although this engine was closely related to the historic Merlin it was not itself successful, and frequently failed. Manchesters served with eleven RAF squadrons and as an aeroplane the type clearly had great possibilities. The engines were the trouble, and the natural decision was taken to fit four Merlins in their place. The result was an aircraft once described by the chief of RAF Bomber Command as the greatest single factor in winning the Second World War. Lancasters were first used to lay mines, on 3 March 1942, but they were mainly employed thereafter in the bombing of Germany. Cities and

The most famous of Britain's four-engined bombers was the Avro Lancaster. Towards the end of the war this type was adapted to carry the 22,000-lb 'earthquake' bomb.

war installations suffered in devastating raids. The historic breaching of the Mohne and Eder dams, the sinking of the battleship *Tirpitz* and the destruction of the Bielefeld viaduct were all the work of Lancasters. Unlike the Stirling and Halifax, the Lancaster inherited from the Manchester a bomb bay which can truly be described as cavernous, and this was used to full advantage. Originally intended to take bombs of up to 4,000 lb, it was progressively adapted to 8,000-lb and 12,000-lb bombs, and eventually the 22,000-lb Grand Slam 'earthquake' bomb. The most astonishing weapon of all was the special and very secret 'spinning drum' bomb used by the Dambusters, concerning whose exploits a

film was made. These bombs were designed by Mr (later Sir) Barnes Wallis, who was also responsible for the geodetic form of construction and the Grand Slam bomb.

There were several versions of the Lancaster, but as it was a classic type a general description may be given.

The airframe was of all-metal construction, as was common at the period. The wing was set at mid position on the fuselage, which was a deep, compact structure of oval cross-section. The backbone of the fuselage was formed by pairs of longerons, or fore-and-aft members, which supported the floor on cross-beams and formed the roof of the bomb bay. The two mainwheels of the undercarriage retracted into the inner engine nacelles but the tailwheel was fixed. Each of the four nacelles contained an oil tank, and there were six petrol tanks in the wings. Power-driven gun turrets were generally fitted in the nose, in a dorsal position not far ahead of the tail, and in the tail itself. The first two turrets had two Browning rifle-calibre guns and the tail turret four. Ammunition for the rear turret was delivered along tracks from boxes in the fuselage. The crew numbered seven. The bomb-aimer's station was in the extreme nose, below the front turret. Raised above the forward fuselage was a large transparent enclosure, or canopy, with the pilot seated forward at the port side. Behind him was the navigator's station and behind this the radio operator's station. A walkway extended along the entire length of the fuselage. The crew stations were extensively protected by armour plating and were supplied with oxygen for high-altitude operation. Equipment included a dinghy carried in the wing. This was automatically released and inflated in an emergency alighting in the sea but could also be operated by hand. The layout of the entire fuselage can be studied in detail at the Imperial War Museum in London.

In the volume on *The World's Fighters* the statement is made that the de Havilland Mosquito was 'the second most versatile aircraft of the war', and that assessment may be repeated here with even greater emphasis, for it was originally designed as a bomber. It has already been noted also that there was an amazingly close relationship between the Mosquito and the D.H.4, but this relationship was closer than has been generally realised. Before his death in 1965 Sir Geoffrey de Havilland recalled a fateful meeting with Air Marshal Sir Wilfrid Freeman, Chief Executive at the Air Ministry, after his proposals for a new bomber had been coldly received by earlier officials of that Ministry. He said: 'I had known Freeman since the early days of the 1914 War and had always liked him. He was far more than a very successful Air Force officer, he had technical knowledge much above the average, and in discussion was helpful and without bias. I had stayed a short time at his headquarters in France when he was in charge of a squadron of D.H.4s and I felt he would appreciate a modern version of that successful machine. It needed only one meeting with this wise and far-sighted man to discuss our plans and to get his full approval and blessing for the Mosquito.'

Although, as already noted, the Mosquito shared with the D.H.4 the features of wooden construction, a Rolls-Royce powerplant and a crew of two, it was, of course, very much more than a modern

Beauty, efficiency and adaptability were characteristics of the de Havilland Mosquito. This is a B Mk IV bomber. Note the sighting panel in the nose.

version of the earlier bomber. It was, in fact, a very beautiful twin-engined mid-wing monoplane with its two Merlin engines carried in long nacelles under a sharply tapering wing. In order to reduce drag the radiators were mounted not in the engine nacelles, as, for example, on the Lancaster, but were buried in the wing, between the nacelles and fuselage. In a military sense the most remarkable feature was that there was no armament whatever: this bomber was to depend for its protection on sheer speed. That this protection was effective was proved by the fact that, towards the end of the war, the Mosquito loss rate was only one in two thousand sorties. The task of opposing fighters was made all the more difficult because the Mosquitoes were flying at between 30,000 and 40,000 ft.

The value of such a remarkable bomber would not, of course, be great unless it could carry a worthwhile load of bombs. The first bomber version to go into service carried four 500-lb bombs, or double the load of the Blenheim, but more than fifty Mk IVs were specially adapted to carry a single 4,000-lb blockbuster. The same type of bomb could be carried by the later Mk XVI, which had improved Merlin engines to enable it to operate for lengthy periods at about 40,000 ft. This meant providing it with a pressurised cabin, that is, one in which the air pressure was kept at a comfortable level however low the pressure outside, due to the great height.

Never had there been a bomber like the Mosquito; but attention must now be turned to another very remarkable bomber, the American Boeing B-17, briefly introduced in an earlier chapter. Although bombers of this type are chiefly associated with their massive high-altitude attacks on targets in Occupied Europe, their use in this manner was never foreseen when the first Model 299 flew across the American continent at 252 mph, as already recorded. It has also been recorded that the name Flying Fortress was at first not merited because the armament proved inadequate. The development of the B-17's armament was truly spectacular and was first marked by the introduction of the B-17E, which carried heavy machine-guns (Browning 0·5-in, or 'fifty caliber' as they were known to the men who manned them) in a tail position; a ventral ball turret (of spherical form); and a turret in the upper part of the nose. Later developments had a chin turret, in the lower part of the nose, and cheek mountings· on either side of the nose. Other guns were added, to a total of eight or more.

Although the B-17 carried a much lighter bomb load than, for instance, the Lancaster, it could operate at much greater heights. Flying in daylight and in formation, the 'Forts' were able to give each other covering fire, and many terrible battles were fought out with German fighters.

Just as the British Lancaster had a companion type in the Halifax, so did the B-17 go into battle together with the Consolidated B-24, or Liberator. Though designed in 1939 as an advance on the B-17, this bomber did not, in service, show any spectacular improvement on the earlier machine except in range. This meant that, although the Liberator shared with the B-17 in the historic attacks on Occupied Europe it achieved an even greater distinction in operations over the Pacific, where its long range was of particular value. This range – 2,850 miles was the figure attained by the B-24D – was achieved largely by the use of a new type of wing called the Davis wing, after its inventor. The wing was set high on the fuselage and was of very high aspect ratio. Such a wing has always been favoured for long-range aircraft (those operating below the speed of sound, at least), and the Davis wing had the additional advantage of being a high-lift wing, that is, one lifting a heavy weight for one of its area. This meant that it could be set at a small angle of attack, or angle of incidence, these terms denoting the angle relative to the air through which the wing was travelling. Thus drag was reduced, enabling the range to be increased still further, as less power and less petrol were required to propel the aircraft through the air.

There were numerous versions of the Boeing B-17 Flying Fortress: ▶
this is a B-17G. Note machine-guns in nose, dorsal, ventral and tail
positions.

Together with the Boeing B-17, the Consolidated B-24 Liberator formed the backbone of America's bomber force in World War II.

Many different versions of the Liberator were built, and, as on the B-17, armament was continually increased.

Two other companion bombers were the twin-engined North American B-25 Mitchell and the Martin B-26 Marauder. The B-25 was named after Brig-Gen 'Billy' Mitchell, who played a very spectacular part in the development of American bombers between the wars by challenging the US Navy to offer one of its ships as a target for his small force of early Martins. The Navy made available some captured German vessels and Mitchell's bombers sank a submarine and a cruiser. Attacks on a battleship, the *Ostfriesland*, were successful only when a new type of 2,000-lb bomb was used.

The B-25, which carried Mitchell's name throughout the war, was used in every field of operations, or theatre of war. On 18 April 1942 a force of sixteen Mitchells, led by Lieut-Col 'Jimmy' Doolittle, made one of the most dramatic raids of the war when, after being launched from the aircraft-carrier *Hornet* (although never intended to be so launched) they dropped bombs on Tokyo.

The Mitchell carried 3,000 lb of bombs and was well armed, though not especially fast. It was well-liked by its crews and, both during and after the war, was used by several air forces.

The Martin Marauder was a fine-looking bomber with a very clean, if somewhat plump, fuselage. This bomber at first gained a very bad name, largely by reason of the large numbers of accidents in which it was involved. The main reason for these was the very high wing loading, that is the weight of the aircraft related to the area of the wing, which meant that the landing speed was also high. Later the wing area was increased, and the Marauder gave a good account of itself.

Two other Martin twin-engined bombers, which were used in lesser numbers, and mainly by the RAF, were the Maryland and Baltimore. An uncommon feature was the fitting of four fixed guns in the wing, a feature which associated them closely with the attack class, as mentioned in the Introduction.

For its size the North American B-25 Mitchell carried very heavy armament. This version had guns in the nose, in a dorsal turret, on the fuselage sides and in the tail.

A type in the same class was the Douglas Boston, originally known as the DB-7 and ordered by France and Britain. This was a particularly fine example of an aircraft which, although widely used as a bomber, had been designed with the low-level attack of ground targets very much in mind. Being fast and manoeuvrable it also made a good fighter, and as related in a companion volume was used as such under the name Havoc.

If the Mosquito is acknowledged to be the finest small bomber of the Second World War then it would be difficult to deny a similar honour among the larger bombers to the Boeing B-29 Superfortress. Sadly, this fine aeroplane is remembered today chiefly because of the two atomic bomb attacks made by aircraft of the type on Japan. The targets were Hiroshima (6 August 1945) and Nagasaki (14 August 1945).

Technically the B-29 marked a new departure in bomber development because it was the first large bomber with pressurised crew accommodation to enter service in large numbers. This feature, together with a very efficient wing of high aspect ratio, and the massive power of its four Wright

The photographer must have been very 'quick on the trigger' to secure this picture of a Boeing B-29 Superfortress delivering its load.

R-3350 air-cooled radial engines, enabled it to fly at heights around 30,000 ft and to achieve a range of about 4,000 miles. The armament was very advanced, as was appropriate on such a bomber, being concentrated in four remote-controlled turrets, each housing two 0·5-in machine-guns, disposed two above and two below the fuselage. There were three additional guns in the tail. The turrets were controlled from sighting blisters, taking the form of transparent enclosures, in the sides and top of the fuselage.

The number of B-29s produced was 2,848, and contracts for more than 5,000 additional bombers

of the type were cancelled when Japan surrendered in August 1945. So excellent was the design that the Russians made a copy of it, which went into service as the Tu-4. The copy was made possible by the unintentional landing in the USSR, owing to fuel shortage, of B-29s engaged in bombing raids against Japan. The Tu-4, however, came too late for use in the Second World War, and it now remains to describe the Soviet bombers which did see service in that conflict.

Although the fact was little known outside the Soviet Union until after the war, the Soviet Air Force had in service a type of large four-engined bomber which was not only notable in design but which made many raids deep into Germany. These raids included an attack on Berlin in the summer of 1941. The bomber concerned was known as the Petlyakov Pe-8, because V. M. Petlyakov was responsible for preparing the aircraft for production. The basic design was, in fact, the work of the team led by the famous Soviet designer A. N. Tupolev, some of whose earlier bombers were mentioned in a preceding chapter.

The Pe-8 was especially interesting in respect of its engines and armament. The original Tupolev design was itself remarkable for the fact that, although apparently having four engines, it was actually five-engined, the fifth engine being mounted in the fuselage to drive a supercharger system for the other four. This system was abandoned in production aircraft, but some of these, including a number which raided Germany, were nevertheless remarkable in having diesel engines, operating on the same principle as those installed in London buses. This type of engine gave excellent fuel economy, and the diesel-engined Pe-8 had a range of over 4,800 miles when carrying 4,400 lb of bombs. The interesting point concerning the armament was that two of the guns were installed in the rear ends of the inner engine nacelles.

Most of the Soviet bombers were twin-engined, and prominent among these were types designed both by Tupolev and Petlyakov. The first of the Tupolev types, the SB-2, might well have been introduced in an earlier chapter, for it entered service in 1936 and was in action in the Spanish Civil War, but it is included here as one of the best-known bombers of the Second World War, and also for comparison with the later Tu-2. In terms of performance the SB-2 was comparable with the Bristol Blenheim, though it was considerably larger; but like the Blenheim, Hampden and other bombers of its time it was poorly armed, and was eventually used only at night.

The next type of Tupolev bomber was vastly superior, having a speed of 342 mph as well as a heavy armament. Known as the Tu-2, this type entered production in 1942, though it was built only in relatively small numbers because the Russians were already committed to very large production of the Petlyakov Pe-2, later mentioned. The Tu-2 was armed with 12·7-mm guns, one each in two dorsal positions (an unusual feature) and one in a ventral position very far aft (also unusual). Additional armament in the form of two forward-firing cannon fixed in the wing was intended mainly for ground attack.

Although, like the German Junkers Ju 88, it had braking surfaces to restrict its speed in a dive and thus enable it to be used for dive-bombing (the bombs being aimed by pointing the machine at the target), the Petlyakov Pe-2 is rightly considered here because it could also be used for level bombing. Perhaps its most unusual feature was the method of carrying the bombs: a load of 440 lb could be carried in the fuselage bomb bay; provision for an additional 220 lb was made in the rear of the engine nacelles; and 880 lb could be slung under the wings. If only large bombs were required the load, consisting of four 550-lb or two 1,100-lb bombs, was carried under the wings.

Two other types of Soviet bomber call for mention, though the first of these was merely a development of the Ilyushin DB-3 referred to in an earlier chapter. Called the DB-3F, or sometimes Il-4, this was to become perhaps the most famous Soviet bomber of all, for it served throughout the war on every front on which the Russians fought the Germans and their allies. The DB-3F was noticeably different from the DB-3 in having a completely redesigned forward fuselage. Whereas the earlier machine had a blunt nose with a gun turret the improved version had a tapering nose into which was let a rotatable circular gun mounting which formed the extreme tip. A similar mounting was

used on the Heinkel He 111, and the DB-3F may be considered as the opposite number of that widely used German bomber, though, as already remarked, it was a wholly Soviet design. When metal became short many parts were made of wood.

The other bomber to be mentioned was a comparatively little known and little used one bearing a name which has a particular appeal to English eyes. This was the Archangelskii Ar-2, and it was really a development of the Tupolev SB-2. The main difference was a smaller wing.

	Span	Length	Crew	Loaded weight	Maximum speed	Service ceiling	Armament
GREAT BRITAIN							
Armstrong Whitworth Whitley V	84′ 0″	70′ 6″	4	28,000 lb	222 mph	17,600 ft	5 r-c m-g
Bristol Blenheim I	56′ 4″	39′ 9″	3	12,500 lb	260 mph	27,250 ft	2–3 r-c m-g
Handley Page Hampden	69′ 2″	53′ 7″	3	18,756 lb	254 mph	19,000 ft	4–6 r-c m-g
Vickers Wellington IC	86′ 2″	64′ 7″	4	25,800 lb	235 mph	19,000 ft	6 r-c m-g
Fairey Battle	54′ 0″	52′ 2″	3	10,792 lb	241 mph	23,500 ft	2–4 r-c m-g
Short Stirling III	99′ 1″	87′ 3″	7	70,000 lb	270 mph	17,000 ft	8 r-c m-g
Handley Page Halifax I	98′ 10″	70′ 1″	7	60,000 lb	265 mph	22,800 ft	6–8 r-c m-g
Avro Lancaster I	102′ 0″	69′ 6″	7	63,000 lb	281 mph	23,500 ft	8 r-c m-g
de Havilland Mosquito XVI	54′ 2″	41′ 6″	2	23,000 lb	415 mph	40,000 ft	nil

	Span	Length	Crew	Loaded weight	Maximum speed	Service ceiling	Armament
USA							
Boeing B-17F	103′ 9″	74′ 9″	6	55,000 lb	299 mph	37,500 ft	8 h m-g
Consolidated B-24D	110′ 0″	66′ 4″	6	60,000 lb	303 mph	32,000 ft	8 h m-g
North American B-25J	67′ 7″	52′ 11″	4	35,000 lb	272 mph	24,200 ft	7 h m-g
Martin B-26B	65′ 0″	58′ 3″	4	34,000 lb	317 mph	23,500 ft	7 h m-g
Boeing B-29A	141′ 3″	99′ 0″	10	141,100 lb	358 mph	31,850 ft	11 h m-g
USSR							
Petlyakov Pe-8	131′ 0″	73′ 8″	5	68,500 lb	275 mph	32,950 ft	2 c 2 h m-g+2 r-c m-g
Petlyakov Pe-2	56′ 3″	41′ 4″	2	18,750 lb	335 mph	28,870 ft	2 h m-g+2 r-c m-g
Tupolev Tu-2	61′ 10″	45′ 4″	4	28,220 lb	341 mph	31,150 ft	2 c+2 h m-g
Ilyushin DB-3F	70′ 4″	48′ 7″	4	22,170 lb	276 mph	29,500 ft	3 h m-g

8

The Second World War:
Italy, Germany, Japan

The principal Italian bombers used in the war of 1939–45 were described in an earlier chapter, but one type remains to be included here because this was the only one comparable with such classic four-engined types as the Lancaster, Halifax, B-17 and B-24. This bomber was the Piaggio P.108B, a type which was first in action over Gibraltar in 1942. Later in the war Bruno Mussolini, son of the Italian dictator, was killed in a bomber of this same type.

Technically the most interesting feature of the P.108B was its armament of eight heavy machine-guns and their arrangement. Four of the guns were in dorsal and ventral turrets, but the remaining four

were installed in two pairs in a very remarkable manner. Each pair was in a turret in each of the outboard engine nacelles, over the leading edge of the wing. They were sighted from positions in the fuselage, and, being so far out along the wing, commanded a very wide field of fire.

The three great German bomber-producing companies in the Second World War were Dornier, Heinkel and Junkers, all of which, as already shown, were gaining experience during the mid-1930s. The Dornier Do 23 was noted as representing a sort of half-way mark, both in time and in terms of speed; but during the late 1930s Dornier were developing a secret bomber in the design of which there were certainly no half-way measures. This was the Do 17, the existence and speed of which was made known to the world in a very spectacular way.

In July 1937 there was held at Zürich in Switzerland the International Military Aircraft Competition, where a star performer was the new French Dewoitine D.510 single-seat fighter. The drama of the occasion can well be imagined when, in the Circuit of the Alps race, this fighter, and others of its generation, were quite outstripped by a new German twin-engined bomber. Though this was officially called Do 17, it quickly became known as the 'Flying Pencil', because of its very slender appearance when seen from the side. This slenderness was not so evident when the aircraft was seen in plan form, that is from below or above, because of the way in which the wing merged into the fuselage. A fact not then appreciated, and one little known even today, is that the Do 17 had been originally designed not as a bomber but as a very fast six-seat transport. Another fact that was not known at the time was that the Do 17 which appeared at Zürich was a specially prepared specimen and was much faster than the ordinary bombers of the type then being built for the German Air Force. Nevertheless, these were remarkable aeroplanes, as the present writer well recalls, having been

An unusual view of a Dornier Do 17Z, showing how the crew were grouped in the nose. This feature was common in German bombers.

specially privileged to see them in production at the Dornier works on the shores of Lake Constance.

As development of the Do 17 proceeded, and military requirements respecting armament and the dispositions of the crew members became more clearly defined, the new bomber gradually suffered the same fate as many other military aeroplanes; its original beautiful shape began to sprout excrescences, and the Do 17Z, which was the model commonly used against England in the Battle of Britain, differed in many ways from the new aeroplane which had startled the world at Zürich. The

Do 17Z had a completely new forward fuselage, in which the crew of four could work more efficiently, for accommodation was formerly very cramped. This resulted in the fuselage having a blunt entry, or nose portion, which, although it improved the military effectiveness of the aircraft, or made it a better bomber, at the same time robbed it of its former cleanness of line, and speed inevitably suffered. Nor was the new nose rounded, but was composed largely of flat panels, somewhat resembling in this respect the Bristol Blenheim. Another alteration which further detracted from appearance and speed was the fitting of Bramo Fafnir air-cooled radial engines instead of the Daimler-Benz DB 601 liquid-cooled inline engines which might otherwise have been fitted. One reason for this change was the very heavy demands made on production of the liquid-cooled engines by the Messerschmitt fighters; but although the air-cooled engines chosen were less powerful than the DB 601, and presented more resistance to the air, the Do 17Z still had a speed of over 250 mph.

The designation Do 215 applied to a generally similar bomber originally intended for export but also used by the German Air Force. Production-type Do 215s were fitted with DB 601 engines, which increased the speed to about 290 mph.

The next Dornier bomber, the Do 217, was a considerably larger aircraft, although it resembled the Do 17Z and Do 215 in having the crew grouped in the nose. The first version to go into general service was the Do 217E and this had the new and very powerful BMW 801 fourteen-cylinder air-cooled radial engines. These delivered over 1,500 hp each, whereas the Fafnirs in the Do 17Z gave no more than 1,000 hp.

After the Do 217E came the exceptionally interesting Do 217K which had a new, very deep and rounded nose. The main point of interest, however, is that some aircraft of the type had a greatly increased wing span and carried two of the very secret Fritz X or Hs 293 guided bombs for attacks on shipping. These were very special bombs indeed, and were the forerunners of the stand-off bombs of later years. As its name suggests, a bomb of this type allows the aircraft launching it to stand off, or keep away from, a heavily defended target, and yet to deliver the bomb accurately. The Fritz X, or FX, bomb, was a development of an ordinary type of heavy armour-piercing bomb having four wings, or fins, and a tail. It was controlled by radio or by signals transmitted over a wire, and the controller could follow its path by observing a flare or light in the tail. The Hs 293 was in the form of a little aeroplane and was propelled by a rocket motor attached beneath it. It was radio-controlled and was lit up

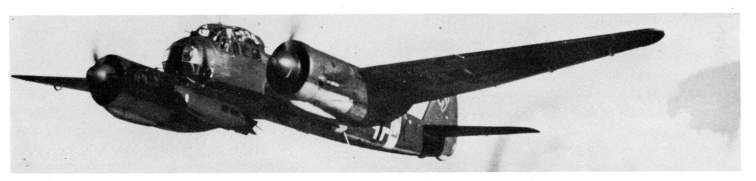

Behind the lower gun position of this Junkers Ju 88 the tail fins of a large bomb are visible.

like the Fritz X. It was generally known as a glider bomb, but, as stated, had its own rocket to propel it.

It must be mentioned that some Do 217Es were used to bring the new bombs up to operational status, that is to make them fit for service, and also to train special crews in their use.

In the book *The World's Fighters* it is mentioned that the Junkers Ju 88 was the most versatile aircraft of the Second World War; but it was originally designed as a bomber. Early development followed the same pattern as in the case of the Do 17, a very clean design being somewhat marred by the requirement of grouping a crew of four closely together in the nose. The nose of the Ju 88A bomber, which was the standard version at the outbreak of war and in the Battle of Britain, was, in fact very similar to that of the Do 17Z.

A truly first-class military aeroplane must, of course, possess more than a good performance, which can usually be related to its external appearance. It must, at the same time, be a safe and pleasant aircraft to fly, and, of very great importance in wartime, it must be easy to produce in large numbers. The design of the new Junkers bomber was prepared with the last requirement very much in mind, and the building of Ju 88s, both as complete aircraft and in components, or parts, was spread over many factories and continued throughout the duration of the war.

One of the most interesting features of the Ju 88 bomber was the fitting beneath the wing, outboard of the engine nacelles, of air brakes or dive brakes. These somewhat resembled farm gates, and were hinged at the front so that they could be lowered to present resistance to the air in a steep diving attack. This restricted the speed, which meant that no excessive strain was put on the strength of the aircraft and that the pilot was able to take accurate aim by pointing the machine in the direction of the target. For use in dive-bombing the pilot had a special sight, which could be swung aside when not in use in order not to obstruct his view. The heavier types of bomb were carried under the wings, between the engine nacelles and fuselage, and lighter bombs inside the fuselage.

It must be emphasised at this point that although it was equipped for dive-bombing the Ju 88 was not a specialised dive-bomber, like the notorious Ju 87 Stuka; provision was also made for a type of bombsight which enabled the bombs to be released in level flight.

Yet another unusual feature of the Ju 88 was the use of annular radiators, or radiators of circular form, for the two Junkers Jumo 211 engines, resulting in a very neat type of power egg. If additional power was required to enable the new bomber to take-off in a short distance with a very heavy load, external rocket packs could be fitted. The term pack in this connection means that after use the entire installation could be jettisoned, or released, and be lowered to the ground by parachute. This meant not only that the aircraft was not encum-

bered with the extra drag of the packs but that the packs themselves could be used again.

The last bomber version of this fine Junkers aircraft was the Ju 88S, in which a very determined effort was made to increase the speed sufficiently to enable the bomber to elude enemy fighters even in daylight. Weight and drag were saved wherever possible. Power was increased not only by fitting the latest types of engine but by injecting nitrous oxide gas, or 'laughing gas', into the supercharger to provide additional oxygen for burning and thus increase the power delivered. This system could only be used for a short period, to give an extra burst of speed over a heavily defended area to evade attack by fighters. In a bomber of today this special capability of developing an extremely high speed for a short period is known as dash performance.

So efficient was the basic Ju 88 design that a new type, the Ju 188, was developed from it. This had a completely new nose and sharply pointed wings of greater span. Purely bomber versions of this type were relatively little used.

Much earlier in this book reference was made to the Ju 86 bomber of the inter-war years: it was stated that the early aircraft of this type were not especially notable but that later developments proved very remarkable indeed. These developments were the Ju 86P and Ju 86R, both having a wing of greatly increased span (the span of the R version was 105 ft, or about 30 ft greater than originally) and both having a pressure cabin for a crew of two only. The use of highly supercharged diesel engines combined with the sacrificing of armament and other equipment and the great span and area of the wing conferred on these bombers an altogether exceptionally high service ceiling, the figure for the Ju 86R being over 47,000 ft. This meant that these special developments of an old bomber, which was itself developed from a transport aeroplane, could sail over enemy territory immune from attack by the latest enemy fighters, even when these were stripped of some armament to save weight and were specially prepared in other ways. Although only a light bomb load was carried, the nuisance value of the special Ju 86s was never in doubt.

The Heinkel bombers were of two types, He 111 and He 177. The first of these was very extensively used throughout the war and remained in service with the Spanish Air Force until the late 1960s. A number of Spanish He 111s were used for the making of the film *The Battle of Britain*. The larger He 177 was far less successful.

The He 111 was briefly mentioned in an earlier chapter, and the earlier versions might well have been included there. Discussion of its development, however, has been reserved for the present occasion because this bomber provides a very striking instance of how a good basic design can be steadily improved over the years.

The first prototype of the He 111 made its first flight early in 1935. It was a strikingly beautiful aeroplane with two BMW twelve-cylinder liquid-cooled engines mounted forward of a wing of elliptical form, similar in design to the wing later developed for the British Spitfire fighter. The new bomber was built in great secrecy, and the first aircraft of the general type that was demonstrated for the Press, in January 1936, was fitted out as a transport for ten passengers. Because the fuselage was so beautifully slender the seating was very cramped. The bomb bay was arranged as a smoking compartment for four passengers. At that time production of the true bomber version was already under way, and He 111Bs were ready to serve with the famous Condor Legion in the Spanish Civil War during 1937. These bombers were fitted with the new Daimler-Benz DB 600 engines of inverted-vee type, that is a vee-type engine with cylinders beneath the crankcase instead of above it as was usual.

In the He 111F a very noticeable change was made: the graceful insect-like elliptical wing was changed for one having straight edges. This wing was found to have roughly the same efficiency as

Glimpsed between the revolving propeller blades of this Heinkel He 111 are carriers for large bombs. Smaller bombs were carried internally.

the original type but was easier to build, and, as already remarked, ease of construction is an important consideration in any military aircraft.

By the time Germany went to war in 1939 nearly a thousand He 111s had been built, and by the early spring of that year the production effort was concentrated on a new version known as the He 111P. This was the version which was extensively used against Poland and in the Battle of Britain. In having three rifle-calibre machine-guns the He 111P was similarly armed to its predecessors; but the guns were arranged in a different manner. The gun in the nose was in a transparent hemispherical mount-

ing which was offset to starboard so that the view obtainable by the pilot, who was seated to port in the largely transparent nose, should not be impaired. There was a second gun at the end of a transparent dorsal enclosure, and the third was in a ventral 'bathtub', which had replaced the retractable dustbin turret of earlier versions. In the Spanish Civil War the armament of three rifle-calibre machine-guns had proved adequate because opposition was relatively light; but experience in the Second World War showed how ineffective it really was, and the number of guns, and in some instances the calibre also, was increased.

Versions of the He 111 were very numerous, but the general efficiency of the type may be judged from these figures for the He 111P: maximum speed about 250 mph without bomb load, 202 mph with bomb load; maximum bomb load about 4,400 lb. Not all the bombs carried by He 111s were of the conventional high-explosive or incendiary type, for towards the end of the war flying bombs of the kind used against London and other centres were air-launched from bombers of this type. Only one flying bomb was carried at a time, this being hung from the port wing between the fuselage and engine nacelle.

The story of the much larger He 177 is one of continuing technical difficulties and political in-decision which need not be related in detail. It may be mentioned, however, that the structure of the aircraft was very heavy because, notwithstanding its size (the wing span was over 100 ft), the duties originally included dive-bombing. Other difficulties were connected with the engines, and in respect of these the type was especially interesting, for whereas it appeared to have only two engines it did, in fact, have four. These were mounted in two pairs in two nacelles. The two engines in each pair were coupled together to drive a single propeller. One reason for using this arrangement was that existing engines could be used instead of developing an entirely new engine of very great power. Troubles with the coupled engines persisted until the end of the war, not the least of these being a tendency for the engines to catch fire. Towards the end of the war efforts were made to adapt the bomber to have four separate engines of ordinary type, and one such development was undertaken by the German-controlled Farman factory in Paris. The new bomber was called He 274A, but the prototype had not been flown when the Germans had to evacuate the French capital.

Although comparatively little known, the last type of German bomber to be mentioned here was perhaps the most revolutionary bomber of all, for it was the first jet-propelled bomber to go into service. The significance of this remarkable aircraft, the Arado Ar 234, has in some degree been obscured by the wide publicity received by the Messerschmitt Me 262 which was pressed into service as a bomber although designed as a fighter. The Ar 234, on the other hand, was specifically intended for bombing duties, although it was also used for reconnaissance.

Of all the Ar 234's remarkable features, the most remarkable of all was the fitting of turbojet engines. This form of engine propels an aircraft by jet re-action, which means that the engine, and the aeroplane on which it is fixed, reacts to the rearward squirting of a stream of hot gases by moving forward.

The propulsive power thus generated is measured as thrust rather than horsepower, as in a piston engine, and although the early turbojets, as installed in the Ar 234, delivered very low thrusts by modern standards, they nevertheless enabled much higher speeds to be attained than formerly.

Another striking feature of the new Arado bomber, which entered service late in 1944, was its very compact and clean design, partly owing to the fact that it was a single-seater, the pilot sitting in the extreme nose of the fuselage. The cockpit was pressurised by air tapped from the turbojets and the pilot sat in an ejection seat. This type of seat literally fired the occupant out of the aircraft in emergency and became necessary because baling out with a parachute became extremely difficult, if not impossible, at the very high speeds obtainable with jet propulsion.

The first true bomber version of the Ar 234 to enter service was the Ar 234B-2 and this could carry a bomb load of up to 3,300 lb, one 1,100-lb bomb being attached under the fuselage and a similar bomb under each of the two nacelles housing the turbojets. A bombsight was mounted between the pilot's feet. In some aircraft of the type two 20-mm cannon were fixed in the fuselage to fire aft, and these guns were aimed by a very ingenious means. The bombsight already mentioned was for bombing

in level flight. If the aircraft were to be used for dive-bombing a special type of sight was fitted which embodied a periscope sticking out from the roof of the cockpit. This periscope could be turned rearwards for sighting the guns.

Much more could be written about the Ar 234. Although it was never used in great numbers at least it has now been accorded its rightful place in the history of bombers.

After such a remarkable machine the Japanese bombers of the Second World War will appear as an unexciting collection; but they must be given their place, especially as there are facts of uncommon interest concerning certain types.

All the Japanese bombers to be mentioned were monoplanes with two air-cooled radial engines; Japan used no four-engined bombers during the entire war. The principal constructor was Mitsubishi, and the bombers produced by this company were of three types, all of them of later design than the G3M, which, as previously recorded, took part in the historic attacks on HMS *Repulse* and *Prince of Wales*. The first of the new bombers was the Ki-21, which, although it had a very good performance, proved, like several other bombers of its time, to have too light an armament. This became especially apparent when aircraft of the type met British Hurricane fighters over Burma. The firepower of the last version was improved by installing a heavy machine-gun in a dorsal turret instead of the rifle-calibre gun formerly mounted in the same position.

A later Mitsubishi bomber, the G4M, was built in greater numbers than any other Japanese bomber and was notable for its extremely long range. The range of some versions was far in excess of 3,000 miles. This fine bomber, however, suffered severely because the immense load of petrol necessary to achieve its great range was carried in unprotected tanks and was thus very vulnerable to attack by fighters. American pilots called it the 'one-shot lighter'. It was, however, much better armed than the Ki-21, the defensive weapons including a 20-mm cannon in the tail. Bombers of this type shared with G3Ms in sinking the British ships earlier mentioned.

A considerable number of G4Ms were specially equipped to carry and launch the Ohka piloted bomb. This took the form of a small rocket-propelled aeroplane which was deliberately flown into its target by its pilot, who thus sacrificed his life. The warhead, or explosive part, of the piloted bomb occupied nearly one third of the length of the fuselage and weighed 2,645 lb. Great damage was inflicted by this terrible weapon.

Whereas the G3M and G4M were operated by the Japanese Navy, the next Mitsubishi bomber was an Army type, as was the earlier Ki-21. The new bomber, the Ki-67 Hiryu, or Flying Dragon, did not come into service until quite late in the war, but proved to be unquestionably the finest of all the Japanese Army bombers. With its two Mitsubishi Ha-104 eighteen-cylinder engines it achieved a speed of 334 mph, and although the bomb load was comparatively light (1,100 lb normal, 1,760 lb maximum) the armament was formidable, consisting of four heavy machine-guns and a 20-mm cannon.

Each of the three types of Japanese bomber remaining to be mentioned was made by a different company. The Kawasaki Ki-48 was a far lighter and smaller machine than the types already described and was used not only for level bombing but for dive-bombing also. The dive brakes were similar to those of the German Ju 88. The normal bomb load was only 660 lb, but when used for suicide attacks, as were several other types of Japanese aircraft, the bomb load was increased to 1,765 lb. As its name suggests, a suicide attack involved flying the aircraft deliberately into the target and sacrificing the pilot.

The Nakajima Ki-49 Donryu, or Storm Dragon, was designed to replace the Mitsubishi Ki-21, which it never really did. Although superior in performance and in other respects to the older machine its maximum bomb load of 2,205 lb was no better and it was more difficult to fly.

The last of the Japanese bombers was a very fine one indeed. This was a Naval type, known as the Yokosuka P1Y Ginga, or Milky Way, and not only was it fast (340 mph maximum), well armed (three heavy machine-guns was a typical installation) but it had a high rate of climb and excellent manoeuvrability.

During 1945 one P1Y was used to test an early form of jet-propulsion engine, but Japan was never to build a jet-propelled bomber.

	Span	Length	Crew	Loaded weight	Maximum speed	Service ceiling	Armament
ITALY							
Piaggio P.108B	105' 0"	73' 1"	7	65,885 lb	267 mph	19,680 ft	8 h m-g
GERMANY							
Dornier Do 17Z	59' 1"	51' 10"	4	19,480 lb	263 mph	26,740 ft	4 r-c m-g
Dornier Do 217E	62' 4"	60' 10"	4	33,730 lb	320 mph	29,530 ft	1 c+2 h m-g+3 r-c m-g
Junkers Ju 88A	60' 3"	47' 1"	4	22,840 lb	280 mph	26,250 ft	3–5 r-c m-g
Junkers Ju 88S	65' 7"	48' 9"	3	30,400 lb	379 mph	38,000 ft	1 h m-g
Junkers Ju 86R	105' 0"	54' 0"	2	25,420 lb	261 mph	47,250 ft	nil or 1 r-c m-g
Heinkel He 111P	74' 2"	53' 9"	5	29,760 lb	247 mph	26,250 ft	5–6 r-c m-g
Heinkel He 177A	103' 2"	66' 11"	5	66,140 lb	317 mph	22,960 ft	1 c+3 h m-g+3 r-c m-g
Arado Ar 234B	46' 3"	41' 5"	1	20,610 lb	461 mph	37,700 ft	nil or 2 c
JAPAN							
Mitsubishi Ki-21	73' 10"	52' 6"	5	17,450 lb	268 mph	28,200 ft	6 r-c m-g
Mitsubishi G4M	82' 0"	65' 7"	7	27,560 lb	272 mph	29,360 ft	2 c+4 r-c m-g
Mitsubishi Ki-67	73' 10"	61' 4"	6	30,350 lb	334 mph	31,000 ft	1 c+4 h m-g
Kawasaki Ki-48	57' 4"	41' 4"	4	13,340 lb	298 mph	31,150 ft	1 h m-g+3 r-c m-g
Nakajima Ki-49	67' 0"	55' 2"	8	25,130 lb	306 mph	30,500 ft	1 c+1 h m-g+2 r-c m-g
Yokosuka P1Y	65' 7"	49' 3"	3	29,760 lb	340 mph	30,800 ft	3 h m-g

9

The Mighty Jets

So immense was the effect of jet propulsion on the design and performance of bombers that the temptation must be resisted to pass over the remaining piston-engined types which call for mention; but as these types include one bomber which was immense in size and importance the story of their development must be told in full.

The last of the British piston-engined bombers was the Avro Lincoln, a development of the Lancaster with greater wing span, more power and increased armament which, on some aircraft of the type, included two 20-mm cannon in a turret. An equivalent type in United States service was the Boeing B-50, a development of the wartime B-29 with more powerful piston engines which gave it a speed of no less than 380 mph. Very extensive and valuable service was rendered by a twin-engined type which had seen service towards the end of the war as the Douglas A-26 (the A signifying attack) but which, when the Martin B-26 Marauder passed out of service in 1948, was given the same designation. These very fine bombers served not only in Korea but in Vietnam also.

The piston-engined bomber mentioned as being immense in size and importance was the Convair B-36, the design of which grew from the realisation that, as the Germans dominated most of Europe, it might become necessary to attack targets in that continent from bases in the USA. The first B-36 did not, in fact, fly until the war was over, but many scores of these great bombers were built in later years. While these were in service the huge Bristol Brabazon airliner was being tested in England, but few people realised that bombers of the same size,

Ten-engined bomber: 'pods' for four turbojet engines, in two pairs, are seen outboard of the six piston engines on this Convair B-36. Wing span was 230 feet.

and much greater in weight, were flying in large numbers every day.

If ever a bomber could be described as fabulous it was the B-36. The wing measured 230 ft in span and was six feet thick. Within this thickness the six great Pratt & Whitney air-cooled engines were completely buried, each driving a pusher propeller. To increase the speed to about 430 mph and the

The Boeing B-47 Stratojet was a very great step forward in bomber design.
This picture shows the unusual engine arrangement, 'bicycle' undercarriage, and parachute to shorten the landing run.

service ceiling to over 45,000 ft four turbojet engines were later fitted beneath the wings. Sixteen 20-mm cannon were mounted in turrets, controlled from two crew compartments which were connected by an 80-ft tunnel. Through this tunnel the crew could move on a wheeled trolley. Even with a heavy bomb load a B-36 could remain in the air for twenty-four hours without being refuelled in flight. This was a means of increasing the range of bombers and other aircraft which was then becoming available. Not without justification was the B-36 known as America's 'big stick'. Compared with some of the rapier-like jet bombers now to be described it was indeed a bludgeon.

The first American jet bomber to enter service was made by the North American company and was called the B-45 Tornado. Although the airframe was quite normal in appearance one extraordinary feature was apparent. This was the mounting beneath each wing of a very broad nacelle. The reason for the great breadth was that in each nacelle were two turbojets, mounted side by side. The Tornado proved a fine aeroplane, much in the tradition of its famous predecessor the Mitchell, and the type remained in service for ten years.

As already noted, the airframe of the Tornado appeared quite normal, but the same could certainly not be said for that of the Boeing B-47 Stratojet, which followed the Tornado into service. Practically every feature of this bomber was entirely new, and among these features the slender sweptback wing was especially remarkable. The effectiveness of wing sweepback in the achievement of high speeds was a German discovery, the benefits of which were quickly realised by the Americans and Russians. Britain lagged far behind in appreciating the value of the swept wing.

The second most remarkable feature of the B-47 was the curious installation of the six turbojets. The nacelles containing these were suspended below the wing, and largely forward of it, on slim attachments which, in front view, resembled stalks. This led to nacelles so mounted being called engine pods, and podded engines became a familiar feature not only on Boeing bombers and transport aeroplanes but on aircraft of other makes also.

A third remarkable feature of the B-47 was its undercarriage, which was in the form of two main units mounted one behind the other, one at each end of the bomb bay, and retracting into the fuselage. To prevent the new bomber from toppling over sideways extra small outrigger wheels were mounted on, and retracted into, the inboard engine pods. These pods were larger than the outboard pair because each one contained not one, but two, turbojets.

Compared with the features described the provision of built-in rockets to provide additional power

for take-off and the fitting in the tail of a drag-producing parachute to help to shorten the landing run seemed quite ordinary. Although the new bomber had to be handled very carefully by its pilots it proved an outstanding aircraft. Many hundreds were built and B-47s continued in first-line service until 1966.

Hardly surprisingly, some of the main features of the B-47 were retained for a new type of very large Boeing bomber, in the design of which the attainment of a very long range was of first importance. This bomber was the B-52 Stratofortress, the first prototype of which flew in 1952 and production of which was completed about ten years later. Until recent years at least a part of the US Air Force's fleet of B-52s was constantly in the air, with weapons in their bomb bays and maps of their targets on the flight deck in the nose of the great fuselage. In the B-52 the two pilots were seated side-by-side whereas in the B-47 they were in tandem.

The last production version was the B-52H, with eight Pratt & Whitney turbofan engines. This type of engine is really a half-way between a turbojet, already described, and a propeller-turbine, described later. The fan part of the name relates to an internal fan which accelerates rearwards a smaller mass of air than the airscrew driven by a propeller-turbine but a greater mass than the stream of hot gases

Beneath the 185-foot wing of this Boeing B-52G Stratofortress are ▶
seen two Hound Dog missiles, pods for the eight turbojet engines,
and fuel tanks.

squirted rearwards by a turbojet. The turbofan is generally the engine favoured when a long range is required together with a high subsonic speed, or speed below the speed of sound. The immense range conferred by the new engines was demonstrated in January 1962, when a B-52 flew 12,519 miles nonstop from Okinawa to Madrid.

Among the weapons carried by the B-52 is a jet-propelled winged missile, or stand-off bomb, called Hound Dog, which can be launched as far as 700 miles from its target. Needless, perhaps, to add, the warhead is atomic, and as the B-52 can carry four such weapons the destructive power of this great bomber can be imagined. In Vietnam, of course, the bombs dropped by B-52s have been of ordinary type, for example, 750-lb high-explosive bombs in great numbers.

The podded engine arrangement introduced by the B-47 and continued by the B-52 was a feature also of a twin-jet bomber, the Douglas B-66 Devastator, which was really a shore-based version of the US Navy's deck-landing A-3 Skywarrior. Although a relatively small bomber, the Devastator had a turret in the tail housing two 20-mm cannon.

Podded engines and armament in the tail were also features of the Convair B-58 Hustler, the first prototype of which was flown in November 1956. In most other respects, however, this bomber differed amazingly from any of its predecessors, and this is not surprising, for the Hustler was the world's first supersonic bomber – a bomber capable of flying above the speed of sound. Here, indeed, was a bomber which could be named in company with the D.H.4, Fox, Mosquito, B-36 and B-47: there was nothing to match it in the world. Not only did this bomber fly above the speed of sound, it flew at more than twice the speed of sound. Moreover, it could fly for long distances, though not at such high speeds. This was demonstrated when a Hustler flew from New York to Paris in just under 3 hr 20 min.

Among the features which made such performance possible was the extremely thin delta wing, that is, a wing roughly triangular in planform. Beneath this were four pods, each containing a General Electric J-79 turbojet, of the latest and most powerful type then being installed in American fighters. But the word pod was also applied to the Hustler in another connection, namely that of weapon pod. This was a very big streamlined container carried beneath the fuselage, one part of it housing an atomic bomb and the remainder the fuel to be consumed on the journey to the target. When this pod had served its purpose it was dropped to save drag. Later a two-component pod was introduced, the larger and lower pod containing fuel and the other both fuel and a bomb.

Hustler was indeed an appropriate name for the world's first supersonic bomber, the Convair B-58.
The array of 'pods' is explained in the text.

Passing reference must now be made to another extraordinary American aircraft, of later and more revolutionary design than the Hustler. This is the swing-wing General Dynamics F-111. Although the F in the designation denotes fighter F-111s have been used in Vietnam as bombers. The truth is that the F-111 falls into the class of aircraft which, as explained in the introductory chapter, would be best considered separately as strike aircraft.

The story of bomber development, in which some remarkably contrasting designs have already been described, remains to be concluded by reviewing the British and Soviet bombers of twenty-five years past.

Some further remarkable contrasts will be apparent.

Britain's first jet bomber was the English Electric Canberra, first flown in May 1949. Like the North American Tornado, which had preceded it by about two years, the Canberra had an airframe of quite conventional appearance; but so excellent did this British bomber prove that it was built under licence in the United States as the Martin B-57 and was exported to several countries. It was a delightful machine to fly and had a degree of manoeuvrability which can truly be described as fighter-like. Like its famous predecessor in RAF service, the Mosquito, it had side-by-side seating for its crew of two; and it was unarmed.

Britain's first jet-propelled bomber, the English Electric Canberra, was so successful that it was built under licence in America. This is a B Mk 6 of No. 101 Squadron, RAF.

Three more types of jet bomber followed the Canberra into RAF service, and these were known as the 'V bombers' because they were all large, unarmed, long-range, high-altitude four-jet aircraft having names beginning with V. The first of these was the Vickers Valiant, which went into service in 1955. This bomber had four Rolls-Royce Avon turbojets, of the type which had proved highly successful in the Canberra, and these engines were mounted in the bulged inner sections of the wing. There was much technical discussion at the time concerning the merits of this arrangement and the American system of podding. If extra thrust were needed for take-off this was provided by two de Havilland Super Sprite rocket engines, which could be fixed under the wing and jettisoned after use. The maximum bomb load of 10,000 lb was a fairly light one, but

the Valiant proved a fine aircraft. Together with Canberras, Valiants were used in the Suez operations of 1956.

The second of the V bombers was the Avro (later Hawker Siddeley) Vulcan, a magnificent-looking delta-wing machine with four of the new Bristol Siddeley Olympus turbojets in a buried installation in the wing. Although the wing was originally of true delta shape, with straight edges, it was later altered to have compound sweep on the leading edge. This meant that the sweepback angle on the inner sections was far less than on the outer sections, resulting in a distinctive kink.

Although unarmed, the Vulcan, like several other bombers of its period, carried special equipment to jam the enemy's radar. This was installed in the tail cone, or rear tip, of the fuselage. A single

Avro Vulcan B Mk 2s. Camouflage, as seen on the nearer machine, was applied to the upper surfaces to render identification more difficult in low-level attacks.

Blue Steel stand-off bomb could be carried.

The Blue Steel bomb was also carried by the third V bomber, the Handley Page Victor, and this bomber likewise had a wing with a kinked leading edge. There were few more points of resemblance, however, for the Victor was the first bomber to have a crescent wing. In this type of wing the angle of sweepback on the leading edge decreases progressively, in the case of the Victor in three distinct stages. One of the advantages of this form of wing was that

the aircraft was easy to land; pilots said, in fact, that the Victor almost landed itself. Early Victors had Bristol Siddeley Sapphire turbojets, but Rolls-Royce Conway turbofans were later fitted.

The first jet bomber to serve with the French (and later Israeli) Air Force was the SO 4050 IIB Vautour (Vulture). This swept-wing twin-jet bomber could carry over 5,000 lb of bombs and had an undercarriage of the type fitted to the Boeing B-47. The crew of two sat in tandem and there was no defensive

Although having two turbojet engines instead of one the Dassault Mirage IV bomber bears a very striking resemblance to the Mirage III fighter. Beneath the fuselage is a circular emplacement for radar and a recessed nuclear weapon.

armament. This bomber could attain supersonic speed in a dive, but far higher speeds were achieved in level flight by a later type of French jet bomber, the Dassault Mirage IV. This was designed to carry the French atomic bomb and generally resembled the Mirage III fighter, though it was larger and had two Atar turbojets instead of one. Even so, the bomber was extremely compact, having a wing span of less than 39 ft. In order to obtain adequate range fuel was carried in every available space, including the tail fin. As in service today this fine delta-wing bomber has a normal range of over 2,000 miles, and during part of its bombing sortie can fly at 1·7 times the speed of sound.

Just as the famous names of Vickers, Avro and Handley Page continued to be associated with bombers long after the Second World War so did the names Ilyushin and Tupolev live on in the Soviet Union.

The first Soviet jet-propelled bomber to go into service in large numbers appears to have been the Ilyushin Il-28, a twin-jet machine closely comparable with the Canberra, though with the very noticeable difference of having a gunner in a heavily protected turret in the tail. For this position two 20-mm cannon are provided. It has been estimated that no fewer than ten thousand Il-28s have been built, and certainly the type is used by many air forces.

Of the Tupolev jet bombers the first appears to have been the Tu-12, a development of the piston-

Although basically of clean design the Tupolev Tu-16 is blemished with blisters for wheel-retraction, radar installations and visual observation. It is probably the world's most heavily armed jet bomber.

engined Tu-2 described earlier. Then came the Tu-14, which generally resembled the Il-28; but neither of these bombers was built in great numbers. This distinction was nevertheless achieved by the Tu-16, a much larger type, quite closely comparable with the Boeing B-47, though with the very notable difference of having two very powerful turbojets instead of six smaller ones. These engines are mounted on the sides of the fuselage, at the roots of the sweptback wing. The Tu-16 is closely related to the Tu-104 airliner and shares with it the unusual method of retracting the mainwheels of the undercarriage. These fold rearwards into two large blisters at the trailing edge of the wing. There are several other excrescences, some of them associated with the heavy armament of cannon. The aircraft takes on an even more untidy appearance when carrying two anti-shipping stand-off bombs under the wing or a single large stand-off bomb under the fuselage.

Great numbers of Tu-16s are in service, together with another type of Tupolev bomber distinguished by its very large size (the span of the sweptback

Unmistakable in appearance, with its two big turbojet engines above the rear fuselage, is the supersonic Tupolev Tu-22. This one has an escort of MiG-21 fighters.

wing is 163 ft) and in having four extremely powerful propeller-turbines. This type of engine has as its main part a gas turbine, as have the turbojet and turbofan, but in this instance it is used to drive a propeller. The Tu-95 has, in fact, eight propellers, for each engine drives two co-axial contra-rotating propellers. This expression means that the propellers are mounted on the same axis, or one immediately behind the other, and that they rotate in opposite directions. With a speed estimated to be over 550 mph, the Tu-95 is beyond doubt the fastest propeller-driven aircraft in the world, its immense size notwithstanding. A very large stand-off bomb can be carried and there is a heavy defensive armament of cannon.

The Soviet equivalent of the supersonic Hustler

is yet another Tupolev bomber, the Tu-22. The most remarkable feature is the installation of the two unusually powerful turbojets above the fuselage at the extreme rear end, where a cannon is also mounted. Bombers of this very modern type have been observed carrying a stand-off bomb.

The last of the Soviet bombers to pass under review, the Myasishchev Mya-4, is another very impressive one, being the Russian equivalent of the Boeing B-52 and somewhat resembling that type in the form of its tandem undercarriage. There is, however, one very obvious difference, in that only four turbojets are fitted instead of eight, and these are mounted in the root sections of the swept-back wing. It is estimated that this great bomber can carry a bomb or bombs weighing 10,000 lb at a speed of 520 mph for a distance of 7,000 miles without being refuelled in flight.

This bomber is already old, having made its first public appearance over Moscow in May 1954; yet the advance it represents over the *Il'ya Muromets* is a measurement of progress in bomber design.

	Span	Length	Crew	Loaded weight	Maximum speed	Service ceiling	Arma-ment
USA							
Convair B-36D	230′ 0″	162′ 1″	10	357,500 lb	439 mph	45,200 ft	16 c
North American B-45	89′ 0″	75′ 4″	4	95,560 lb	580 mph	46,250 ft	2 h m-g
Boeing B-47E	116′ 0″	109′ 10″	3	206,700 lb	606 mph	40,500 ft	2 c
Boeing B-52H	185′ 0″	157′ 7″	10	490,000 lb	630 mph	55,000 ft	2 c
Douglas B-66B	72′ 6″	75′ 2″	3	83,000 lb	620 mph	45,000 ft	2 c
Convair B-58A	56′ 10″	96′ 9″	3	160,000 lb	1,385 mph	60,000 ft	1 c
GREAT BRITAIN							
English Electric Canberra B.6	63′ 11″	65′ 6″	2	55,000 lb	540 mph	48,000 ft	nil
Vickers Valiant	114′ 4″	108′ 3″	3	175,000 lb	540 mph	54,000 ft	nil
Avro Vulcan B.2	111′ 0″	99′ 11″	5	200,000 lb†	645 mph†	60,000 ft†	nil
Handley Page Victor B.2	120′ 0″	114′ 11″	5	200,000 lb†	Mach 0·95†	‡	nil
FRANCE							
SO 4050 Vautour	49′ 7″	52′ 0″	2	45,635 lb	685 mph	50,000 ft	nil
Dassault Mirage IV	38′ 11″	77′ 1″	2	69,665 lb	1,450 mph	65,000 ft	nil
USSR							
Tupolev Tu-16	110′ 0″	120′ 0″	7*	150,000 lb	587 mph	42,650 ft	7 c

* Unconfirmed † Approximate ‡ Data not available

10

Bomber for Tomorrow

When the writing of this book was begun, early in 1970, the future of the bomber was very obscure indeed. Aircraft of this class were becoming vastly expensive to develop and operate, and even in the United States there was much uncertainty. It was known, however, that in November 1969 requests for design proposals for a new bomber had been issued to certain manufacturers. At one stage the aircraft was called the AMSA (advanced manned strategic aircraft), but the designation B-1A later became official. The airframe manufacturers approached were Boeing, General Dynamics and North American Rockwell. In respect of engines Pratt & Whitney and General Electric were consulted.

During June 1970 came the news that a contract worth $2,300 million (£960 million), to design,

develop and test five B-1As had been awarded to North American Rockwell. The engine contract, alone worth $400 million (£167 million), was placed with General Electric. It was further disclosed that orders for B-1As, to replace the B-52s and B-58s of the United States Air Force, were likely to total $12,000 million (£5,000 million) over a ten-year period.

Spending of this order naturally involves an extremely advanced bomber indeed, and the B-1A should be able to fly at three times the speed of sound. This speed would be attained at a great height, but the new bomber is expected also to be capable of supersonic speed in the dense air at a very low level. The engines will be of turbofan type.

America's mighty new bombers should be coming into service in 1977–78, and eventually they could number 200–240.

Technical details of the B-1A are, of course, secret, but the placing of the contract with North American Rockwell is seen as being of great significance, for North American Aviation, Inc, which merged with Rockwell-Standard Corporation to form the company named earlier, has unique experience in the building of extremely fast aeroplanes. Bestknown of these was the X-15 research aircraft, three of which were built some years ago. These fantastic 'manned missiles' flew at 6·7 times the speed of sound and attained altitudes of about 67 miles. Of equal interest in the present connection with bombers was the construction of two XB-70 Valkyries, the first of which flew in 1964 and the second in 1965. The aircraft were purely experimental, although at one time it was thought that bombers of the type might replace the B-52s and B-58s. The fuselage was 185 ft long, although the span of the delta wing was only 105 ft. Speeds of about 1,980 mph were attained, and two features which helped to make the Valkyrie as fantastic in appearance as in performance were the foreplane, or small wing, attached to the nose of the fuselage, and the grouping of the six tubojets in a massive box-like structure.

Beyond question, the Valkyries were the most amazing bombers ever built, but, like several other remarkable aircraft of this class, have received no previous mention because they never entered service. This review of operational bombers may, however, be fittingly concluded with brief reference to three other experimental might-have-beens. These were Britain's Vickers Windsor, which had a wing like a Spitfire's and a wheel retracting into each of its four engine nacelles; Germany's Junkers Ju 287, with its swept-forward wing and turbojets attached to the sides of the fuselage; and America's Northrop Flying Wing, which was exactly what its name denoted, and had no fuselage at all.

The design features which will make the B-1A America's 'bomber for tomorrow' are as yet unknown.

FURTHER READING

British Aeroplanes 1914–1918, J. M. Bruce, Putnam, London, 1957.

British Bomber since 1914, The, Peter Lewis, Putnam, London, 1967.

Combat Aircraft of the World, edited and compiled by John W. R. Taylor, Ebury Press and Michael Joseph, London, 1969.

Jane's All the World's Aircraft, edited by John W. R. Taylor, Sampson Low Marston & Co Ltd, London. Annual.

Warplanes of the Second World War: Bombers (Three volumes), William Green, Macdonald, London, 1967, 1968.

INDEX OF PRINCIPAL AIRCRAFT